The Provincial American

The Provincial American

And Other Papers

By
Meredith Nicholson

Essay Index Reprint Series

BOOKS FOR LIBRARIES PRESS
FREEPORT, NEW YORK

First Published 1912
Reprinted 1971

INTERNATIONAL STANDARD BOOK NUMBER:
0-8369-2211-5

LIBRARY OF CONGRESS CATALOG CARD NUMBER:
79-152205

PRINTED IN THE UNITED STATES OF AMERICA

To
George Edward Woodberry
Guide, Counselor
And the most inspiring of Friends
This Volume is Dedicated
With grateful and affectionate
Regard

Indianapolis, September 1912.

Contents

The Provincial American
And Other Papers

The Provincial American

Viola. What country, friends, is this?
Captain.   This is Illyria, lady.
Viola. And what should I do in Illyria?
        My brother he is in Elysium.
                                        Twelfth Night.

I AM a provincial American. My forebears
were farmers or country-town folk. They
followed the long trail over the mountains out
of Virginia and North Carolina, with brief so-
journs in western Pennsylvania and Kentucky.
My parents were born, the one in Kentucky,
the other in Indiana, within two and four hours
of the spot where I pen these reflections, and I
had voted before I saw the sea or any Eastern
city.

In attempting to illustrate the provincial
point of view out of my own experiences I am
moved by no wish to celebrate either the
Hoosier commonwealth—which has not lacked
nobler advertisement—or myself; but by the
hope that I may cheer many who, flung by fate
upon the world's byways, shuffle and shrink

3

The Provincial American

under the reproach of their metropolitan brethren.

Mr. George Ade has said, speaking of our fresh-water colleges, that Purdue University, his own *alma mater*, offers everything that Harvard provides except the sound of *a* as in " father." I have been told that I speak our *lingua rustica* only slightly corrupted by urban contacts. Anywhere east of Buffalo I should be known as a Westerner; I could not disguise myself if I would. I find that I am most comfortable in a town whose population does not exceed a fifth of a million, — a place in which men may relinquish their seats in the street car to women without having their motives questioned, and where one calls the stamp-clerk at the post-office by his first name.

I

Across a hill-slope that knew my childhood, a bugle's grieving melody used to float often through the summer twilight. A highway lay hidden in the little vale below, and beyond it the unknown musician was quite concealed, and was never visible to the world I knew. Those

4

The Provincial American

trumpetings have lingered always in my memory, and color my recollections of all that was near and dear in those days. Men who had left camp and field for the soberer routine of civil life were not yet fully domesticated. My bugler was merely solacing himself for lost joys by recurring to the vocabulary of the trumpet. I am confident that he enjoyed himself; and I am equally sure that his trumpetings peopled the dusk for me with great captains and mighty armies, and touched with a certain militancy all my youthful dreaming.

No American boy born during or immediately after the Civil War can have escaped in those years the vivid impressions derived from the sight and speech of men who had fought its battles, or women who had known its terror and grief. Chief among my playthings on that peaceful hillside was the sword my father had borne at Shiloh and on to the sea; and I remember, too, his uniform coat and sash and epaulets and the tattered guidon of his battery, that, falling to my lot as toys, yet imparted to my childish consciousness a sense of what war had been. The young imagination was kindled in

those days by many and great names. Lincoln,
Grant, and Sherman were among the first lisp-
ings of Northern children of my generation; and
in the little town where I was born lived men
who had spoken with them face to face. I did
not know, until I sought them later for myself,
the fairy-tales that are every child's birthright;
and I imagine that children of my generation
heard less of

> "old, unhappy, far-off things,
> And battles long ago," —

and more of the men and incidents of contemporaneous history. Great spirits still on earth
were sojourning. I saw several times, in his last
years, the iron-willed Hoosier War Governor,
Oliver P. Morton. By the time I was ten, a
broader field of observation opening through
my parents' removal to the state capital, I had
myself beheld Grant and Sherman; and every
day I passed in the street men who had been
partners with them in the great, heroic, sad,
splendid struggle. These things I set down as
a background for the observations that follow,
— less as text than as point of departure; yet I

6

The Provincial American

believe that bugler, sounding "charge" and "retreat" and "taps" in the dusk, and those trappings of war beneath whose weight I strutted upon that hillside, did much toward establishing in me a certain habit of mind. From that hillside I have since ineluctably viewed my country and my countrymen and the larger world.

Emerson records Thoreau's belief that "the flora of Massachusetts embraced almost all the important plants of America, — most of the oaks, most of the willows, the best pines, the ash, the maple, the beech, the nuts. He returned Kane's 'Arctic Voyage' to a friend of whom he had borrowed it, with the remark that most of the phenomena noted might be observed in Concord."

The complacency of the provincial mind is due less, I believe, to stupidity and ignorance, than to the fact that every American county is in a sense complete, a political and social unit, in which the sovereign rights of a free people are expressed by the court-house and town hall, spiritual freedom by the village church-spire, and hope and aspiration in the school-house. Every reader of American fiction, particularly

The Provincial American

in the realm of the short story, must have observed the great variety of quaint and racy characters disclosed. These are the *dramatis personæ* of that great American novel which some one has said is being written in installments. Writers of fiction hear constantly of characters who would be well worth their study. In reading two recent novels that penetrate to the heart of provincial life, Mr. White's "A Certain Rich Man" and Mrs. Watts's "Nathan Burke," I felt that the characters depicted might, with unimportant exceptions, have been found almost anywhere in those American States that shared the common history of Kansas and Ohio. Mr. Winston Churchill, in his admirable novels of New England, has shown how closely the purely local is allied to the universal.

When "David Harum" appeared, characters similar to the hero of that novel were reported in every part of the country. I rarely visit a town that has not its cracker-barrel philosopher, or a poet who would shine but for the callous heart of the magazine editor, or an artist of supreme though unrecognized talent, or a forensic orator of wonderful powers, or a mechanical

The Provincial American

genius whose inventions are bound to revolu-
tionize the industrial world. In Maine, in the
back room of a shop whose windows looked
down upon a tidal river, I have listened to tariff
discussions in the dialect of Hosea Biglow; and
a few weeks later have heard farmers along the
un-salt Wabash debating the same questions
from a point of view that revealed no masted
ships or pine woods, with a new sense of the fine
tolerance and sanity and reasonableness of our
American people. Mr. James Whitcomb Riley,
one of our shrewdest students of provincial character, introduced me one day to a friend of his
in a village near Indianapolis who bore a striking resemblance to Abraham Lincoln, and who
had something of Lincoln's gift for humorous
narration. This man kept a country store, and
his attitude toward his customers, and "trade"
in general, was delicious in its drollery. Men
said to be "like Lincoln" have not been rare in
the Mississippi Valley, and politicians have been
known to encourage belief in the resemblance.

Colonel Higginson once said that in the Cam-
bridge of his youth any member of the Harvard
faculty could answer any question within the

range of human knowledge; whereas in these days of specialization some man can answer the question, but it may take a week's investigation to find him. In "our town" — "a poor virgin, sir, an ill-favored thing, sir, but mine own!" — I dare say it was possible in that *post-bellum* era to find men competent to deal with almost any problem. These were mainly men of humble beginnings and all essentially the product of our American provinces. I should like to set down briefly the ineffaceable impression some of these characters left upon me. I am precluded by a variety of considerations from extending this recital. The rich field of education I ignore altogether; and I may mention only those who have gone. As it is beside my purpose to prove that mine own people are other than typical of those of most American communities, I check my exuberance. Sad, indeed, the offending if I should protest too much!

II

In the days when the bugle still mourned across the vale, Lew Wallace was a citizen of my native town of Crawfordsville. There he

The Provincial American

had amused himself, in the years immediately
before the civil conflict, in drilling a company of
"Algerian Zouaves" known as the "Mont-
gomery Guards," of which my father was a
member, and this was the nucleus of the Elev-
enth Indiana Regiment which Wallace commanded in the early months of the war. It is
not, however, of Wallace's military services
that I wish to speak now, nor of his writings,
but of the man himself as I knew him later
at the capital, at a time when, in the neighborhood of the federal building at Indianapolis, any
boy might satisfy his longing for heroes with a
sight of many of our Hoosier Olympians. He was
of medium height, erect, dark to swarthiness,
with finely chiseled features and keen black eyes,
with manners the most courtly, and a voice
unusually musical and haunting. His appearance, his tastes, his manner, were strikingly
Oriental.

He had a strong theatric instinct, and his life
was filled with drama — with melodrama, even.
His curiosity led him into the study of many
subjects, most of them remote from the affairs
of his day. He was both dreamer and man of

action; he could be "idler than the idlest
flowers," yet his occupations were many and
various. He was an aristocrat and a democrat;
he was wise and temperate, whimsical and inju-
dicious in a breath. As a youth he had seen
visions, and as an old man he dreamed dreams.
The mysticism in him was deep-planted, and
he was always a little aloof, a man apart. His
capacity for detachment was like that of Sir
Richard Burton, who, at a great company given
in his honor, was found alone poring over a puz-
zling Arabic manuscript in an obscure corner of
the house. Wallace, like Burton, would have
reached Mecca, if chance had led him to that
adventure.

Wallace dabbled in politics without ever
being a politician; and I might add that he
practiced law without ever being, by any high
standard, a lawyer. He once spoke of the law as
"that most detestable of human occupations."
First and last he tried his hand at all the arts.
He painted a little; he moulded a little in clay;
he knew something of music and played the
violin; he made three essays in romance. As
boy and man he went soldiering; he was a civil

The Provincial American

governor, and later a minister to Turkey. In
view of his sympathetic interest in Eastern life
and character, nothing could have been more
appropriate than his appointment to Constanti-
nople. The Sultan Abdul Hamid, harassed and
anxious, used to send for him at odd hours of
the night to come and talk to him, and offered
him on his retirement a number of positions in
the Turkish Government.

With all this rich experience of the larger
world, he remained the simplest of natures. He
was as interested in a new fishing-tackle as in a
new book, and carried both to his houseboat on
the Kankakee, where, at odd moments, he re-
touched a manuscript for the press, or discussed politics with the natives. Here was a
man who could talk of the "Song of Roland" as
zestfully as though it had just been reported
from the telegraph-office.

I frankly confess that I never met him without a thrill, even in his last years and when the
ardor of my youthful hero-worship may be said
to have passed. He was an exotic, our Hoosier
Arab, our story-teller of the bazaars. When
I saw him in his last illness, it was as though

The Provincial American

I looked upon a gray sheik about to fare forth unawed toward unmapped oases.

No lesson of the Civil War was more striking than that taught by the swift transitions of our citizen soldiery from civil to military life, and back again. This impressed me as a boy, and I used to wonder, as I passed my heroes on their peaceful errands in the street, why they had put down the sword when there must still be work somewhere for fighting men to do. The judge of the federal court at this time was Walter Q. Gresham, brevetted brigadier-general, who was destined later to adorn the Cabinets of Presidents of two political parties. He was cordial and magnetic; his were the handsomest and friendliest of brown eyes, and a noble gravity spoke in them. Among the lawyers who practiced before him were Benjamin Harrison and Thomas A. Hendricks, who became respectively President and Vice-President.

Those Hoosiers who admired Gresham ardently were often less devotedly attached to Harrison, who lacked Gresham's warmth and charm. General Harrison was akin to the Covenanters who bore both Bible and sword

The Provincial American

into battle. His eminence in the law was due to his deep learning in its history and philosophy. Short of stature, and without grace of person, — with a voice pitched rather high, — he was a remarkably interesting and persuasive speaker. If I may so put it, his political speeches were addressed as to a trial judge rather than to a jury, his appeal being to reason and not to passion or prejudice. He could, in rapid flights of campaigning, speak to many audiences in a day without repeating himself. He was measured and urbane; his discourses abounded in apt illustrations; he was never dull. He never stooped to pietistic clap-trap, or chanted the jaunty chauvinism that has so often caused the Hoosier stars to blink.

Among the Democratic leaders of that period, Hendricks was one of the ablest, and a man of many attractive qualities. His dignity was always impressive, and his appearance suggested the statesman of an earlier time. It is one of immortality's harsh ironies that a man who was a gentleman, and who stood moreover pretty squarely for the policies that it pleased him to defend, should be published to the world

in a bronze effigy in his own city as a bandy-
legged and tottering tramp, in a frock coat that
never was on sea or land.

Joseph E. McDonald, a Senator in Congress,
was held in affectionate regard by a wide con-
stituency. He was an independent and vigorous
character who never lost a certain raciness and
tang. On my first timid venture into the fabled
East I rode with him in a day-coach from
Washington to New York on a slow train. At
some point he saw a peddler of fried oysters on a
station platform, alighted to make a purchase,
and ate his luncheon quite democratically from
the paper parcel in his car seat. He convoyed
me across the ferry, asked where I expected to
stop, and explained that he did not care for
the European plan himself; he liked, he said,
to have "full swing at a bill of fare."

I used often to look upon the towering form
of Daniel W. Voorhees, whom Sulgrove, an
Indiana journalist with a gift for translating
Macaulay into Hoosierese, had named "The
Tall Sycamore of the Wabash." In a crowded
hotel lobby I can still see him, cloaked and silk-
hatted, the centre of the throng, and my strict

upbringing in the antagonistic political faith did
not diminish my admiration for his eloquence.

Such were some of the characters who came
and went in the streets of our provincial capital
in those days.

III

In discussions under captions similar to mine
it is often maintained that railways, telegraphs,
telephones, and newspapers are so knitting us
together, that soon we shall all be keyed to a
metropolitan pitch. The proof adduced in support of this is the most trivial, but it strikes
me as wholly undesirable that we should all be
ironed out and conventionalized. In the matter
of dress, for example, the women of our town
used to take their fashions from "Godey's" and
"Peterson's" *via* Cincinnati; but now that we
are only eighteen hours from New York, with
a well-traveled path from the Wabash to Paris,
my counselors among the elders declare that
the tone of our society — if I may use so peril-
ous a word — has changed little from our good
old black alpaca days. The hobble skirt re-
ceives prompt consideration in the "Main"
street of any town, and is viewed with frank

The Provincial American

curiosity, but it is only a one day's wonder. A lively runaway or the barbaric yawp of a new street fakir may dethrone it at any time.

New York and Boston tailors solicit custom among us semi-annually, but nothing is so stubborn as our provincial distrust of fine raiment. I looked with awe, in my boyhood, upon a pair of mammoth blue jeans trousers that were flung high from a flagstaff in the centre of Indianapolis, in derision of a Democratic candidate for governor, James D. Williams, who was addicted to the wearing of jeans. The Democrats sagaciously accepted the challenge, made "honest blue jeans" the battle-cry, and defeated Benjamin Harrison, the "kid-glove" candidate of the Republicans. Harmless demagoguery this, or bad judgment on the part of the Republicans; and yet I dare say that if the sartorial issue should again become acute in our politics the banner of bifurcated jeans would triumph now as then. A Hoosier statesman who to-day occupies high office once explained to me his refusal of sugar for his coffee by remarking that he did n't like to waste sugar that way; he wanted to keep it for his lettuce! I do not urge sugared lettuce as symbolizing our higher provincialism, but mayonnaise may be poison to men who are nevertheless competent to construe and administer law.

It is much more significant that we are all thinking about the same things at the same time, than that Farnam Street, Omaha, and Fifth Avenue, New York, should vibrate to the same shade of necktie. The distribution of periodicals is so managed that California and Maine cut the leaves of their magazines on the same day. Rural free delivery has hitched the farmer's wagon to the telegraph-office, and you can't buy his wife's butter now until he has scanned the produce market in his newspaper. This immediacy of contact does not alter the provincial point of view. New York and Texas, Oregon and Florida will continue to see things at different angles, and it is for the good of all of us that this is so. We have no national political, social, or intellectual centre. There is no "season" in New York, as in London, during which all persons distinguished in any of these particulars meet on common ground. Washington is our nearest approach to such a meeting-place,

The Provincial American

but it offers only short vistas. We of the country visit Boston for the symphony, or New York for the opera, or Washington to view the government machine at work, but nowhere do interesting people representative of all our ninety millions ever assemble under one roof. All our capitals are, as Lowell put it, "fractional," and we shall hardly have a centre while our country is so nearly a continent.

Nothing in our political system could be wiser than our dispersion into provinces. Sweep from the map the lines that divide the States and we should huddle like sheep suddenly deprived of the protection of known walls and flung upon the open prairie. State lines and local pride are in themselves a pledge of stability. The elasticity of our system makes possible a variety of governmental experiments by which the whole country profits. We should all rejoice that the parochial mind is so open, so eager, so earnest, so tolerant. Even the most buckramed conservative on the eastern coast-line, scornful of the political follies of our far-lying provinces, must view with some interest the dallyings of Oregon with the Referendum, and of Des

The Provincial American

Moines with the Commission System. If Milwaukee wishes to try socialism, the rest of us need not complain. Democracy will cease to be democracy when all its problems are solved and everybody votes the same ticket.

States that produce the most cranks are prodigal of the corn that pays the dividends on the railroads the cranks despise. Indiana's amiable feeling toward New York is not altered by her sister's rejection or acceptance of the direct primary, a benevolent device of noblest intention, under which, not long ago, in my own commonwealth, my fellow citizens expressed their distrust of me with unmistakable emphasis. It is no great matter, but in open convention also I have perished by the sword. Nothing can thwart the chastening hand of a righteous people.

All passes; humor alone is the touchstone of democracy. I search the newspapers daily for tidings of Kansas, and in the ways of Oklahoma I find delight. The Emporia "Gazette" is quite as patriotic as the Springfield "Republican" or the New York "Post," and to my own taste, far less depressing. I subscribed for a year to

The Provincial American

the Charleston "News and Courier," and was saddened by the tameness of its sentiments; for I remember (it must have been in 1883) the shrinking horror with which I saw daily in the Indiana Republican organ a quotation from Wade Hampton to the effect that "these are the same principles for which Lee and Jackson fought four years on Virginia's soil." Most of us are entertained when Colonel Watterson rises to speak for Kentucky and invokes the star-eyed goddess. When we call the roll of the States, if Malvolio answer for any, let us suffer him in patience and rejoice in his yellow stockings. "God give them wisdom that have it; and those that are fools, let them use their talents."

Every community has its dissenters, protestants, kickers, cranks; the more the merrier. My town has not lacked impressive examples, and I early formed a high resolve to strive for membership in their execrated company. George W. Julian, — one of the noblest of Hoosiers, — who had been the Free-Soil candidate for Vice-President in 1852, a delegate to the first Republican convention, five times a member of Congress, a supporter of Greeley's candidacy, and a Democrat in the consulship of Cleveland, was a familiar figure in our streets. In 1884 I was dusting law-books in an office where mug-wumpery flourished, and where the iniquities of the tariff, Matthew Arnold's theological opinions, and the writings of Darwin, Spencer, and Huxley were discussed at intervals in the days' business.

IV

Many complain that we Americans give too much time to politics, but there could be no safer outlet for that "added drop of nervous fluid" which Colonel Higginson found in us and turned over to Matthew Arnold for further analysis. No doubt many voices will cry in the wilderness before we reach the promised land. A people which has been fed on the Bible is bound to hear the rumble of Pharaoh's chariots. It is in the blood to resent the oppressor's wrong, the proud man's contumely. The winter evenings are long on the prairies, and we must always be fashioning a crown for Cæsar or rehearsing his funeral rites. No great danger can ever seriously menace the nation so long as the remotest citizen clings to his faith that he is a part of the

23

governmental mechanism and can at any time throw it out of adjustment if it does n't run to suit him. He can go into the court-house and see the men he helped to place in office; or if they were chosen in spite of him, he pays his taxes just the same and waits for another chance to turn the rascals out.

Mr. Bryce wrote: "This tendency to acquiescence and submission; this sense of the insignificance of individual effort, this belief that the affairs of men are swayed by large forces whose movement may be studied but cannot be turned, I have ventured to call the Fatalism of the Multitude." It is, I should say, one of the most encouraging phenomena of the score of years that has elapsed since Mr. Bryce's "American Commonwealth" appeared, that we have grown much less conscious of the crushing weight of the mass. It has been with something of a child's surprise in his ultimate successful manipulation of a toy whose mechanism had baffled him that we have begun to realize that, after all, the individual counts. The pressure of the mass will yet be felt, but in spite of its persistence there are abundant signs that

24

The Provincial American

the individual is asserting himself more and more, and even the undeniable acceptance of collectivist ideas in many quarters helps to prove it. With all our faults and defaults of understanding, — populism, free silver, Coxey's army, and the rest of it, — we of the West have not done so badly. Be not impatient with the young man Absalom; the mule knows his way to the oak tree!

Blaine lost Indiana in 1884; Bryan failed thrice to carry it. The campaign of 1910 in Indiana was remarkable for the stubbornness of "silent" voters, who listened respectfully to the orators but left the managers of both parties in the air as to their intentions. In the Indiana Democratic State Convention of 1910 a gentleman was furiously hissed for ten minutes amid a scene of wildest tumult; but the cause he advocated won, and the ticket nominated in that memorable convention succeeded in November. Within fifty years Ohio, Indiana, and Illinois have sent to Washington seven Presidents, elected for ten terms. Without discussing the value of their public services it may be said that it has been an important demonstra-

The Provincial American

tion to our Mid-Western people of the closeness
of their ties with the nation, that so many men
of their own soil have been chosen to the seat of
the Presidents; and it is creditable to Maine
and California that they have cheerfully ac-
quiesced. In Lincoln the provincial American
most nobly asserted himself, and any discussion
of the value of provincial life and character in
our politics may well begin and end in him. We
have seen verily that

> "Fishers and choppers and ploughmen
> Shall constitute a state."

Whitman, addressing Grant on his return
from his world's tour, declared that it was not
that the hero had walked "with kings with even
pace the round world's promenade"; —

> "But that in foreign lands, in all thy walks with kings,
> Those prairie sovereigns of the West, Kansas, Missouri,
> Illinois,
> Ohio's, Indiana's millions, comrades, farmers, soldiers,
> all to the front,
> Invisibly with thee walking with kings with even pace
> the round world's promenade,
> Were all so justified."

What we miss and what we lack who live in
the provinces seem to me of little weight in the

The Provincial American

scale against our compensations. We slouch,—
we are deficient in the graces, — we are prone
to boast, — and we lack in those fine reticences
that mark the cultivated citizen of the metropolis. We like to talk, and we talk our problems
out to a finish. Our commonwealths rose in the
ashes of the hunter's camp-fires, and we are all
a great neighborhood, united in a common understanding of what democracy is, and ani-
mated by ideals of what we want it to be. That
saving humor which is a philosophy of life
flourishes amid the tall corn. We are old enough
now — we of the West — to have built up in
ourselves a species of wisdom, founded upon
experience, which is a part of the continuing,
unwritten law of democracy. We are less likely
these days to "wobble right" than we are to
stand fast or march forward like an army with
banners.

We provincials are immensely curious. Art,
music, literature, politics — nothing that is of
contemporaneous human interest is alien to us.
If these things don't come to us, we go to them.
We are more truly representative of the American ideal than our metropolitan cousins, be-

The Provincial American

cause (here I lay my head upon the block) we know more about, oh, so many things! We know vastly more about the United States, for one thing. We know what New York is thinking before New York herself knows it, because we visit the metropolis to find out. Sleeping-cars have no terrors for us, and a man who has never been west of Philadelphia seems to us a singularly benighted being. Those of our Western school-teachers who don't see Europe for three hundred dollars every summer get at least as far East as Concord, to be photographed "by the rude bridge that arched the flood."

That fine austerity which the voluble Westerner finds so smothering on the Boston and New York express is lost utterly at Pittsburg. From gentlemen cruising in day-coaches — dull wights who advertise their personal sanitation and literacy by the toothbrush and fountain-pen planted sturdily in their upper left-hand waistcoat pockets — one may learn the most prodigious facts and the philosophy thereof. "Sit over, brother; there's hell to pay in the Balkans," remarks the gentleman who boarded the interurban at Peru or Connersville, and who

The Provincial American

would just as lief discuss the Papacy or child-labor, if revolutions are not to your liking.

In Boston a lady once expressed her surprise that I should be hastening home for Thanksgiving Day. This, she thought, was a New England festival. More recently I was asked by a Bostonian if I had ever heard of Paul Revere. Nothing is more delightful in us, I think, than our meekness before instruction. We strive to please; all we ask is "to be shown."

Our greatest gain is in leisure and the opportunity to ponder and brood. In all these thousands of country towns live alert and shrewd students of affairs. Where your New Yorker scans headlines as he "commutes" homeward, the villager reaches his own fireside without being shot through a tube, and sits down and reads his newspaper thoroughly. When he repairs to the drug-store to abuse or praise the powers that be, his wife reads the paper, too. A United States Senator from a Middle Western State, making a campaign for renomination preliminary to the primaries, warned the people in rural communities against the newspaper and periodical press with its scandals and heresies. "Wait quietly by your firesides, undisturbed by these false teachings," he said in effect; "then go to your primaries and vote as you have always voted." His opponent won by thirty thousand, — the amiable answer of the little red school-house.

v

A few days ago I visited again my native town. On the slope where I played as a child I listened in vain for the mourning bugle; but on the college campus a bronze tablet commemorative of those sons of Wabash who had fought in the mighty war quickened the old impressions. The college buildings wear a look of age in the gathering dusk.

> "Coldly, sadly descends
> The autumn evening. The field
> Strewn with its dank yellow drifts
> Of withered leaves, and the elms,
> Fade into dimness apace,
> Silent; hardly a shout
> From a few boys late at their play!"

Brave airs of cityhood are apparent in the town, with its paved streets, fine hall and library; and everywhere are wholesome life, com-

The Provincial American

fort, and peace. The train is soon hurrying
through gray fields and dark woodlands. Farm-
houses are disclosed by glowing panes; lanterns
flash fitfully where farmers are making all fast
for the night. The city is reached as great factories are discharging their laborers, and I pass
from the station into a hurrying throng homeward bound. Against the sky looms the dome
of the capitol; the tall shaft of the soldiers'
monument rises ahead of me down the long
street and vanishes starward. Here where forests stood seventy-five years ago, in a State that
has not yet attained its centenary, is realized
much that man has sought through all the ages,
— order, justice, and mercy, kindliness and
good cheer. What we lack we seek, and what
we strive for we shall gain. And of such is the
kingdom of democracy.

Edward Eggleston

Edward Eggleston

THE safest appeal of the defender of realism in fiction continues to be to geography. The old inquiry for the great American novel ignored the persistent expansion by which the American States were multiplying. If the question had not ceased to be a burning issue, the earnest seeker might now be given pause by the recent appearance upon our maps of far-lying islands which must, in due course, add to the perplexity of any who wish to view American life steadily or whole. If we should suddenly vanish, leaving only a solitary Homer to chant us, we might possibly be celebrated adequately in a single epic, but as long as we continue malleable and flexible we shall hardly be "begun, continued, and ended" in a single novel, drama, or poem. He were a much-enduring Ulysses who could touch once at all our ports. Even Walt Whitman, from the top of his omnibus, could not see across the palms of Hawaii or the roofs of Manila; and yet we shall doubtless

35

Edward Eggleston

receive, in due course, bulletins from the Dialect Society with notes on colonial influences in American speech. Thus it is fair to assume that in the nature of things we shall rely more and more on realistic fiction for a federation of the scattered States of this decentralized and diverse land of ours in a literature which shall become our most vivid social history. We cannot be condensed into one or a dozen finished panoramas; he who would know us hereafter must read us in the flashes of the kinetoscope.

Important testimony to the efficacy of an honest and trustworthy realism has passed into the record in the work of Edward Eggleston, our pioneer provincial realist. Eggleston saw early the value of a local literature, and demonstrated that where it may be referred to general judgments, where it interprets the universal heart and conscience, an attentive audience may be found for it. It was his unusual fortune to have combined a personal experience at once varied and novel with a self-acquired education to which he gave the range and breadth of true cultivation, and, in special directions, the precision of scholarship. The primary facts of life

Edward Eggleston

as he knew them in the Indiana of his boyhood took deep hold upon his imagination, and the experiences of that period did much to shape his career. He knew the life of the Ohio Valley at an interesting period of transition. He was not merely a spectator of striking social phenomena; but he might have said, with a degree of truth, *quorum pars magna fui;* for he was a representative of the saving remnant which stood for enlightenment in a dark day in a new land. Literature had not lacked servants in the years of his youth in the Ohio Valley. Many knew in those days the laurel madness; but they went "searching with song the whole world through" with no appreciation of the material that lay ready to their hands at home. Their work drew no strength from the Western soil, but was the savorless fungus of a flabby sentimentalism. It was left for Eggleston, with characteristic independence, to abandon fancy for reality. He never became a great novelist, and yet his homely stories of the early Hoosiers, preserving as they do the acrid bite of the persimmon and the mellow flavor of the pawpaw, strengthen the whole case for a discerning and

37

Edward Eggleston

faithful treatment of local life. What he saw will not be seen again, and when "The Hoosier Schoolmaster" and "Roxy" cease to entertain as fiction they will teach as history.

The assumption in many quarters that "The Hoosier Schoolmaster" was in some measure autobiographical was always very distasteful to Dr. Eggleston, and he entered his denial forcibly whenever occasion offered. His own life was sheltered, and he experienced none of the traditional hardships of the self-made man. He knew at once the companionship of cultivated people and good books. His father, Joseph Cary Eggleston, who removed to Vevay, Indiana, from Virginia in 1832, was an alumnus of William and Mary College, and his mother's family, the Craigs, were well known in southern Indiana, where they were established as early as 1799. Joseph Cary Eggleston served in both houses of the Indiana Legislature, and was defeated for Congress in the election of 1844. His cousin, Miles Cary Eggleston, was a prominent Indiana lawyer, and a judge in the early days, riding the long Whitewater circuit, which then extended through eastern Indiana from the

Edward Eggleston

Ohio to the Michigan border. Edward Eggleston was born at Vevay, December 10, 1837. His boyhood horizons were widened by the removal of his family to New Albany and Madison, by a sojourn in the backwoods of Decatur County, and by thirteen months spent in Amelia County, Virginia, his father's former home. There he saw slavery practiced, and he ever afterward held anti-slavery opinions. There was much to interest an intelligent boy in the Ohio Valley of those years. Reminiscences of the frontiersmen who had redeemed the valley from savagery seasoned fireside talk with the spice of adventure; Clark's conquest had enrolled Vincennes in the list of battles of the Revolution; the battle of Tippecanoe was recent history; and the long rifle was still the inevitable accompaniment of the axe throughout a vast area of Hoosier wilderness. There was, however, in all the towns — Vevay, Brookville, Madison, Vincennes — a cultivated society, and before Edward Eggleston was born a remarkable group of scholars and adventurers had gathered about Robert Owen at New Harmony, in the lower Wabash, and while their experiment in socialism was a dismal failure, they left nevertheless an impression which is still plainly traceable in that region. Abraham Lincoln lived for fourteen years (1816–30) in Spencer County, Indiana, and witnessed there the same procession of the Ohio's argosies which Eggleston watched later in Switzerland County.

Edward Eggleston attended school for not more than eighteen months after his tenth year, and owing to ill health he never entered college, though his father, who died at thirty-four, had provided a scholarship for him. But he knew in his youth a woman of unusual gifts, Mrs. Julia Dumont, who conducted a dame school at Vevay. Mrs. Dumont is the most charming figure in early Indiana history, and Dr. Eggleston's own portrait of her is at once a tribute and an acknowledgment. She wrote much in prose and verse, so that young Eggleston, besides the stimulating atmosphere of his own home, had before him in his formative years a writer of somewhat more than local reputation for his intimate counselor and teacher. His schooling continued to be desultory, but his

Edward Eggleston

curiosity was insatiable, and there was, indeed, no period in which he was not an eager student. His life was rich in those minor felicities of fortune which disclose pure gold to seeing eyes in any soil. He wrote once of the happy chance which brought him to a copy of Milton in a little house where he lodged for a night on the St. Croix River. His account of his first reading of "L'Allegro" is characteristic: "I read it in the freshness of the early morning, and in the freshness of early manhood, sitting by a window embowered with honeysuckles dripping with dew, and overlooking the deep trap-rock dalles through which the dark, pine-stained waters of the St. Croix River run swiftly. Just abreast of the little village the river opened for a space, and there were islands; and a raft, manned by two or three red-shirted men, was emerging from the gorge into the open water. Alternately reading 'L'Allegro' and looking off at the poetic landscape, I was lifted out of the sordid world into a region of imagination and creation. When, two or three hours later, I galloped along the road, here and there overlooking the dalles and river, the glory of a

Edward Eggleston

nature above nature penetrated my being; and Milton's song of joy reverberated still in my thoughts." He was, it may be said, a natural etymologist, and by the time he reached manhood he had acquired a reading knowledge of half a dozen languages. We have glimpses of him as chain-bearer for a surveying party in Minnesota; as walking acrooo country toward Kansas, with an ambition to take a hand in the border troubles; and then once more in Indiana, in his nineteenth year, as an itinerant Methodist minister. He rode a four-week circuit with ten preaching places along the Ohio, his theological training being described by his statement that in those days "Methodist preachers were educated by the old ones telling the young ones all they knew." He turned again to Minnesota to escape malaria, preaching in remote villages to frontiersmen and Indians, and later he ministered to churches in St. Paul and elsewhere. He held, first at Chicago and later at New York, a number of editorial positions, and he occasionally contributed to juvenile periodicals; but these early writings were in no sense remarkable.

42

Edward Eggleston

"The Hoosier Schoolmaster" appeared seri-
ally in "Hearth and Home" in 1871. It was
written in intervals of editorial work and was
a *tour de force* for which the author expected
so little publicity that he gave his characters
the names of persons then living in Switzerland and Decatur counties, Indiana, with no
thought that the story would ever penetrate
to its habitat. But the homely little tale, with
all its crudities and imperfections, made a wide
appeal. It was pirated at once in England; it
was translated into French by "Madame
Blanc," and was published in condensed form
in the "Revue des Deux Mondes"; and later,
with one of Mr. Aldrich's tales and other stories
by Eggleston, in book form. It was translated
into German and Danish also. "Le Maître
d'Ecole de Flat Creek" was the title as set over
into French, and the Hoosier dialect suffered a
sea-change into something rich and strange by
its cruise into French waters. The story depicts
Indiana in its darkest days. The State's illit-
eracy as shown by the census of 1830 was 14.32
per cent as against 5.54 in the neighboring
State of Ohio. The "no lickin','no learnin'"

Edward Eggleston

period which Eggleston describes is thus a matter of statistics; but even before he wrote the old order had changed and Caleb Mills, an alumnus of Dartmouth, had come from New England to lead the Hoosier out of darkness into the light of free schools. The story escaped the oblivion which overtakes most books for the young by reason of its freshness and novelty. It was, indeed, something more than a story for boys, though, like "Tom Sawyer" and "The Story of a Bad Boy," it is listed among books of permanent interest to youth. It shows no unusual gift of invention; its incidents are simple and commonplace; but it daringly essayed a record of local life in a new field, with the aid of a dialect of the people described, and thus became a humble but important pioneer in the development of American fiction. It is true that Bret Harte and Mark Twain had already widened the borders of our literary domain westward; and others, like Longstreet, had turned a few spadefuls of the rich Southern soil; but Harte was of the order of romancers, and Mark Twain was a humorist, while Longstreet, in his "Georgia Scenes," gives only the eccentric and fan-

Edward Eggleston

tastic. Eggleston introduced the Hoosier at the bar of American literature in advance of the Creole of Mr. Cable or the negro of Mr. Page or Mr. Harris, or the mountaineer of Miss Murfree, or the delightful shore-folk of Miss Jewett's Maine.

Several of Eggleston's later Hoosier stories are a valuable testimony to the spiritual unrest of the Ohio Valley pioneers. The early Hoosiers were a peculiarly isolated people, shut in by great woodlands. The news of the world reached them tardily; but they were thrilled by new versions of the Gospel brought to them by adventurous evangelists, whose eloquence made Jerusalem seem much nearer than their own national capital. Heated discussions between the sects supplied in those days an intellectual stimulus greater than that of politics. Questions shook the land which were unknown at Westminster and Rome; they are now well-nigh forgotten in the valley where they were once debated so fiercely. The Rev. Mr. Bosaw and his monotonously sung sermon in "The Hoosier Schoolmaster" are vouched for, and preaching of the same sort has been heard in Indiana at a

Edward Eggleston

much later period than that of which Eggleston wrote. "The End of the World" (1872) describes vividly the extravagant belief of the Millerites, who, in 1842-43, found positive proof in the Book of Daniel that the world's doom was at hand. This tale shows little if any gain in constructive power over the first Hoosier story, and the same must be said of "The Circuit Rider," which portrays the devotion and sacrifice of the hardy evangelists of the Southwest among whom Eggleston had served. "Roxy" (1878) marks an advance; the story flows more easily, and the scrutiny of life is steadier. The scene is Vevay, and he contrasts pleasantly the Swiss and Hoosier villagers, and touches intimately the currents of local religious and political life. Eggleston shows here for the first time a capacity for handling a long story. The characters are of firmer fibre; the note of human passion is deeper, and he communicates to his pages charmingly the atmosphere of his native village, — its quiet streets and pretty gardens, the sunny hills and the broad-flowing river. Vevay is again the scene in "The Hoosier Schoolboy" (1883), which is, however, no worthy successor

Edward Eggleston

to "The Schoolmaster." The workmanship is infinitely superior to that of his first Hoosier tale, but he had lost touch, either with the soil (he had been away from Indiana for more than a decade), or with youth, or with both, and the story is flat and tame. After another long absence he returned to the Western field in which he had been a pioneer, and wrote "The Graysons" (1888), a capital story of Illinois, in which Lincoln is a character. Here and in "The Faith Doctor," a novel of metropolitan life which followed three years later, the surer stroke of maturity is perceptible; and the short stories collected in "Duffles" include "Sister Tabea," a thoroughly artistic bit of work, which he once spoke of as being among the most satisfactory things he had written.

A fault of all of Eggleston's earlier stories is their too serious insistence on the moral they carried — a resort to the Dickens method of including Divine Providence among the *dramatis personæ;* but this is not surprising in one in whom there was, by his own confession, a lifelong struggle "between the lover of literary art

Edward Eggleston

and the religionist, the reformer, the philan-
thropist, the man with a mission." There is
little humor in these tales, — there was doubtless little in the life itself, — but there is abundant good nature. In all he maintains consist-
ently the point of view of the realist, his lapses
being chiefly where the moralist has betrayed
him. There are many pictures which denote his
understanding of the illuminative value of
homely incident in the life he then knew best;
there are the spelling-school, the stirring religious debates, the barbecue, the charivari, the
infare, glimpses of "Tippecanoe and Tyler too,"
and the "Hard Cider" campaign. Those times
rapidly receded; Indiana is one of the older
States now, and but for Eggleston's tales there
would be no trustworthy record of the period
he describes.

Lowell had made American dialect respectable, and had used it as the vehicle for his political gospel; but Eggleston invoked the Hoosier
lingua rustica to aid in the portrayal of a type.
He did not, however, employ dialect with the
minuteness of subsequent writers, notably Mr.
James Whitcomb Riley; but the Southwestern

Edward Eggleston

idiom impressed him, and his preface and notes
in the later edition of "The Schoolmaster" are
invaluable to the student. Dialect remains in
Indiana, as elsewhere, largely a matter of observation and opinion. There has never been a uniform folk-speech peculiar to the people living
within the borders of the State. The Hoosier
dialect, so called, consisting more of elisions and
vulgarized pronunciations than of true idiom,
is spoken wherever the Scotch-Irish influence is
perceptible in the West Central States, notably
in the southern counties of Ohio, Indiana, and
Illinois. It is not to be confounded with the
cruder speech of the "poor-whitey," whose wild
strain in the Hoosier blood was believed by
Eggleston to be an inheritance of the English
bond-slave. There were many vague and baffling elements in the Ohio Valley speech, but
they passed before the specialists of the Dialect
Society could note them. Mr. Riley's Hoosier
is more sophisticated than Eggleston's, and
thirty years of change lie between them,—years
which wholly transformed the State, physically
and socially. It is diverting to have Eggleston's
own statement that the Hoosiers he knew in his

49

Edward Eggleston

youth were wary of New England provincialisms, and that his Virginia father threatened to inflict corporal punishment on his children "if they should ever give the peculiar vowel sound heard in some parts of New England in such words as 'roof' and 'root.'"

While Eggleston grew to manhood on a frontier which had been a great battle-ground, the mere adventurous aspects of this life did not attract him when he sought subjects for his pen; but the culture-history of the people among whom his life fell interested him greatly, and he viewed events habitually with a critical eye. He found, however, that the evolution of society could not be treated satisfactorily in fiction, so he began, in 1880, while abroad, the researches in history which were to occupy him thereafter to the end of his life. His training as a student of social forces had been superior to any that he could have obtained in the colleges accessible to him, for he had seen life in the raw; he had known, on the one hand, the vanishing frontiersmen who founded commonwealths around the hunters' camp-fires; and he had, on the other, witnessed the dawn of a new

Edward Eggleston

era which brought order and enlightenment. He thus became a delver in libraries only after he had scratched under the crust of life itself. While he turned first to the old seaboard colonies in pursuit of his new purpose, he brought to his research an actual knowledge of the beginnings of new States which he had gained in the open. He planned a history of life in the United States on new lines, his main idea being to trace conditions and movements to remotest sources. He collected and studied his material for sixteen years before he published any result of his labors beyond a few magazine papers. "The Beginnings of a Nation" (1896) and "The Transit of Civilization" (1901) are only part of the scheme as originally outlined, but they are complete as far as they go, and are of permanent interest and value. History was not to him a dusty lumber room, but a sunny street where people came and went in their habits as they lived; and thus, in a sense, he applied to history the realism of fiction. He pursued his task with scientific ardor and accuracy, but without fussiness or dullness. His occupations as novelist and editor had been a preparation

51

Edward Eggleston

for his later work, for it was the story quality
that he sought in history, and he wrote with an
editorial eye to what is salient and interesting.
It is doubtful whether equal care has ever been
given to the preparation of any other historical
work in this country. The plan of the books is
in itself admirable, and the exhaustive character of his researches is emphasized by copious
notes, which are hardly less attractive than
the text they amplify and strengthen. He expressed himself with simple adequacy, without flourish, and with a nice economy of words;
but he could, when he chose, throw grace and
charm into his writing. He was, in the best
sense, a humanist. He knew the use of books,
but he vitalized them from a broad knowledge
of life. He had been a minister, preaching a
simple gospel, for he was never a theologian as
the term is understood, but he enlisted zealously in movements for the bettering of mankind, and his influence was unfailingly wholesome and stimulating.

His robust spirit was held in thrall by an in-
valid body, and throughout his life his work was
constantly interrupted by serious illnesses; but

Edward Eggleston

there was about him a certain blitheness; his outlook on life was cheerful and sanguine. He was tremendously in earnest in all his undertakings and accomplished first and last an immense amount of work, — preacher, author, editor, and laborious student, his industry was ceaseless. His tall figure, his fine head with its shock of white hair, caught the attention in any gathering. He was one of the most charming of talkers, leading lightly on from one topic to another. No one who ever heard his voice can forget its depth and resonance. Nothing in our American annals is more interesting or more remarkable than the rise of such men, who appear without warning in all manner of out-of-the-way places and succeed in precisely those fields which environment and opportunity seemingly conspire to fortify most strongly against them. Eggleston possessed in marked degree that self-reliance which Higginson calls the first requisite of a new literature, and through it he earned for himself a place of dignity and honor in American letters.

A Provincial Capital

A Provincial Capital

THE Hoosier is not so deeply wounded by
the assumption in Eastern quarters that
he is a wild man of the woods as by the amiable
condescension of acquaintances at the seaboard, who tell him, when he mildly remon-
strates, that his abnormal sensitiveness is
provincial. This is, indeed, the hardest lot, to
be called a "mudsill" and then rebuked for
talking back! There are, however, several
special insults to which the citizen of Indianapolis is subjected, and these he resents with all
the strength of his being. First among them is
the proneness of many to confuse Indianapolis
and Minneapolis. To the citizen of the Hoosier
capital, Minneapolis seems a remote place, that
can be reached only by passing through Chicago. Still another source of intense annoyance
is the persistent fallacy that Indianapolis is
situated on the Wabash River. There seems to
be something funny about the name of this
pleasant stream, — immortalized in late years

57

A Provincial Capital

by a tuneful balladist, — which a large percentage of the people of Indianapolis have never seen except from a car window. East of Pittsburg the wanderer from Hoosierdom expects to be asked how things are on the Waybosh, — a pronunciation which, by the way, is never heard at home. Still another grievance that has embittered the lives of Indianapolitans is the annoying mispronunciation of the name of their town by benighted outsiders. Rural Hoosiers, in fact, offend the ears of their city cousins with Indianopolis; but it is left usually for the Yankee visitor to say *Injun-*apolis, with a stress on *Injun* which points rather unnecessarily to the day of the war-whoop and scalp-dance.

Indianapolis — like Jerusalem, "a city at unity with itself," where the tribes assemble, and where the seat of judgment is established — is in every sense the capital of all the Hoosiers. With the exception of Boston, it is the largest state capital in the country; and no other American city without water communication is so large. It is distinguished primarily by the essentially American character of its

A Provincial Capital

people. A considerable body of Germans contributed much first and last to its substantial growth, not only by the example of their familiar industry and frugality, but in later years through their intelligent interest in all manner of civic improvement, in general education, and in music and art. Only in the past decade has there been any perceptible drift of undesirable immigrants from southeastern Europe to our city and the problems they create have been met promptly by wise agencies of social service. There was an influx of negroes at the close of the war, and the colored voters (about seventy-five hundred in 1912) add considerably to our political perplexities.

Indiana was admitted as a State in 1816, and the General Assembly, sitting at Corydon in 1821, designated Indianapolis, then a settlement of struggling cabins, as the state capital. The name of the new town was not adopted without a struggle, Tecumseh, Suwarro, and Concord being proposed and supported, while the name finally chosen aroused the hostility of those who declared it unmelodious and etymologically abominable. It is of record that the

59

first mention of the name Indianapolis in the legislature caused great merriment. The town was laid out in broad streets, which were quickly adorned with shade trees that are an abiding testimony to the foresight of the founders. Alexander Ralston, one of the engineers employed in the first survey, had served in a similar capacity at Washington, and the diagonal avenues and the generous breadth of the streets are suggestive of the national capital. The urban landscape lacks variety: the town is perfectly flat, and in old times the mud was intolerable, but the trees are a continuing glory.

Central Indiana was not, in 1820, when the first cabin was built, a region of unalloyed delight. The land was rich, but it was covered with heavy woods, and much of it was under water. Indians still roamed the forests, and the builder of the first cabin was killed by them. There were no roads, and White River, on whose eastern shore the town was built, was navigable only by the smallest craft. Mrs. Beecher, in "From Dawn to Daylight," described the region as it appeared in the forties: "It is a level stretch of land as far as the eye can reach, looking as if one good, thorough rain would transform it into an impassable morass. How the inhabitants contrive to get about in rainy weather, I can't imagine, unless they use stilts. The city itself has been redeemed from this slough, and presents quite a thriving appearance, being very prettily laid out, with a number of fine buildings." Dr. Eggleston, writing in his novel "Roxy" of the same period, lays stress on the saffron hue of the community, the yellow mud seeming to cover all things animate and inanimate.

But the founders possessed faith, courage, and hardihood, and "the capital in the woods" grew steadily. The pioneers were patriotic and religious; their patriotism was, indeed, touched with the zeal of their religion. For many years before the Civil War a parade of the Sunday-school children of the city was the chief feature of every Fourth of July celebration. The founders labored from the first in the interest of morality and enlightenment. The young capital was a converging point for a slender stream of population that bore in from New England, and a broader current that swept westward from the Middle and Southeastern States. There was no sectional feeling in those days. Many of the prominent settlers from Kentucky were Whigs, but a newcomer's church affiliation was of far more importance than his political belief. Membership in a church was a social recommendation in old times, but the importance of religion seemed to diminish as the town passed the two-hundred-thousand mark. Perhaps two hundred thousand is the dead-line — I hope no one will press me too hard to defend this suggestion — beyond which a community loses its pristine sensitiveness to benignant influences; but there was indubitably in the history of our capital a moment at which we became disagreeably conscious that we were no longer a few simple and well-meaning folk who made no social engagements that would interfere with Thursday night prayer meeting, but a corporation of which we were only unconsidered and unimportant members.

The effect of the Civil War upon Indianapolis was immediate and far-reaching. It emphasized, through the centralizing there of the

A Provincial Capital

State's military energy, the fact that it was the capital city, — a fact which until that time had been accepted languidly by the average Hoosier countryman. The presence within the State of an aggressive body of sympathizers with Southern ideas directed attention throughout the country to the energy and resourcefulness of Morton, the War Governor, who pursued the Hoosier Copperheads relentlessly, while raising a great army to send to the seat of war. Again, the intense political bitterness engendered by the war did not end with peace, or with the restoration of good feeling in neighboring States, but continued for twenty-five years more to be a source of political irritation, and, markedly at Indianapolis, a cause of social differentiation. In the minds of many, a Democrat was a Copperhead, and a Copperhead was an evil and odious thing. Referring to the slow death of this feeling, a veteran observer of affairs who had, moreover, supported Mr. Cleveland's candidacy twice, recently said that he had never been able wholly to free himself from this prejudice. But the end really came in 1884, with the reaction against Blaine, which was

A Provincial Capital

nowhere more significant of the flowering of independence than at Indianapolis.

Following the formative period, which may be said to have ended with the Civil War, came an era of prosperity in business, and even of splendor in social matters. Some handsome habitations had been built in the *ante-bellum* days, but they were at once surpassed by the homes which many citizens reared for themselves in the seventies. These remain, as a group, the handsomest residences that have been built at any period in the history of the city. Life had been earnest in the early days, but it now became picturesque. The terms "aristocrats" and "first families" were heard in the community, and something of traditional Southern ampleness and generosity crept into the way of life. No one said *nouveau riche* in those days; the first families were the real thing. No one denied it, and misfortune could not shake or destroy them.

A panic is a stern teacher of humility, and the financial depression that fell upon the country in 1873 drove the lesson home remorselessly at Indianapolis. There had been nothing

A Provincial Capital

equivocal about the boom. Western speculators had not always had a fifty-year-old town to operate in, — the capital of a State, a natural railway centre, — no arid village in a hot prairie, but a real forest city that thundered mightily in the prospectus. There was no sudden collapse; a brave effort was made to ward off the day of reckoning; but this only prolonged the agony. Among the victims there was little whimpering. A thoroughbred has not proved his mettle until he has held up his head in defeat, and the Hoosier aristocrat went down with his flag flying. Those that had suffered the proud man's contumely then came forth to sneer. An old-fashioned butternut Democrat remarked, of a banker who failed, that "no wonder Blank busted when he drove to business in a carriage behind a nigger in uniform." The memory of the hard times lingered long at home and abroad. A town where credit could be so shaken was not, the Eastern insurance companies declared, a safe place for further investments; and in many quarters Indianapolis was not forgiven until an honest, substantial growth had carried the lines of

A Provincial Capital

the city beyond the *terra incognita* of the boom's outer rim.

Many of the striking characteristics of the true Indianapolitan are attributable to those days, when the city's bounds were moved far countryward, to the end that the greatest possible number of investors might enjoy the ownership of town lots. The signal effect of this dark time was to stimulate thrift and bring a new era of caution and conservatism; for there is a good deal of Scotch-Irish in the Hoosier, and he cannot be fooled twice with the same bait. During the period of depression the town lost its zest for gayety. It took its pleasures a little soberly; it was notorious as a town that welcomed theatrical attractions grudgingly, though this attitude must be referred back also to the religious prejudices of the early comers. Your Indianapolitan who has personal knowledge of the panic, or who had listened to the story of it from one who weathered the storm, has never forgotten the discipline of the seventies: though he has reached the promised land, he still remembers the hot sun in the tyrant's brickyards. So con-

66

A Provincial Capital

servatism became the city's rule of life. The panic of 1893 caused scarcely a ripple, and the typical Indianapolis business man to this day is one who minds his barometer carefully.

Indianapolis became a city rather against its will. It liked its own way, and its way was slow; but when the calamity could no longer be averted, it had its trousers creased and its shoes polished, and accepted with good grace the fact that its population had reached two hundred thousand, and that it had crept to a place comfortably near the top in the list of bank clearances. A man who left Indianapolis in 1885, returned in 1912 — the Indianapolitan, like the cat in the ballad, always comes back; he cannot successfully be transplanted — to find himself a stranger in a strange city. Once he knew all the people who rode in chaises; but on his return he found new people flying about in automobiles that cost more than any but the most prosperous citizen earned in the horse-car days; once he had been able to discuss current topics with a passing friend in the middle of Washington Street; now he must duck and dive, and keep an eye

A Provincial Capital

on the policeman if he would make a safe crossing. He is asked to luncheon at a club; in the old days there were no clubs, or they were looked on as iniquitous things; he is carried off to inspect factories which are the largest of their kind in the world. At the railroad yards he watches the loading of machinery for shipment to Russia and Chili, and he is driven over asphalt streets to parks that had not been dreamed of before his term of exile.

Manufacturing is the great business of the city, still sootily advertised on the local countenance in spite of heroic efforts to enforce smoke-abatement ordinances. There are nearly two thousand establishments within its limits where manufacturing in some form is carried on. Many of these rose in the day of natural gas, and it was predicted that when the gas had been exhausted the city would lose them; but the number has increased steadily despite the failure of the gas supply. There are abundant coal-fields within the State, so that the question of fuel will not soon be troublesome. The city enjoys, also, the benefits to be derived from the numerous manufactories in other

A Provincial Capital

towns of central Indiana, many of which maintain administrative offices there. It is not only a good place in which to make things, but a point from which many things may be sold to advantage. Jobbing flourished even before manufacturing attained its present proportions. The jobbers have given the city an enviable reputation for enterprise and fair dealing. When you ask an Indianapolis jobber whether the propinquity of St. Louis, Cincinnati, Chicago, and Cleveland is not against him, he answers that he meets his competitors daily in every part of the country and is not afraid of them.

Indianapolis was long a place of industry, thrift, and comfort, where the simple life was not only possible but necessary. Its social entertainments were of the tamest sort, and the change in this respect has come only within a few years, — with the great wave of growth and prosperity that has wrought a new Indianapolis from the old. If left to itself, the old Indianapolis would never have known a horse show or a carnival, —would never have strewn itself with confetti, or boasted the greatest

A Provincial Capital

automobile speedway in the world; but the
invading time-spirit has rapidly destroyed the
walls of the city of tradition. Business men no
longer go home to dinner at twelve o'clock and
take a nap before returning to work; and the
old amiable habit of visiting for an hour in an
office where ten minutes of business was to be
transacted has passed. A town is at last a city
when sociability has been squeezed out of
business and appointments are arranged a day
in advance by telephone.

The distinguishing quality of Indianapolis
continues, however, to be its simple domestic-
ity. The people are home-loving and home-
keeping. In the early days, when the town was
a rude capital in the wilderness, the citizens
stayed at home perforce; and when the railroad
reached them they did not take readily to
travel. A trip to New York is still a much more
serious event, considered from Indianapolis,
than from Denver or Kansas City. It was an
Omaha young man who was so little appalled
by distance that, having an express frank, he
formed the habit of sending his laundry work
to New York, to assure a certain finish to his

A Provincial Capital

linen that was unattainable at home. The more the Hoosier travels, the more he likes his own town. Only a little while ago an Indianapolis man who had been in New York for a week went to the theatre and saw there a fellow-townsman who had just arrived. He hurried around to greet him at the end of the first act. "Tell me," he exclaimed, "how is everything in old Indianapolis?"

The Hoosiers assemble at Indianapolis in great throngs with slight excuse. In addition to the steam railroads that radiate in every direction interurban traction lines have lately knit new communities into sympathetic relationship with the capital. One may see the real Hoosier in the traction station, — and an ironed-out, brushed and combed Hoosier he is found to be. You may read the names of all the surrounding towns on the big interurban cars that mingle with the local traction traffic. They bring men whose errand is to buy or sell, or who come to play golf on the free course at Riverside Park, or on the private grounds of the Country Club. The country women join their sisters of the city in attacks upon the bar-

A Provincial Capital

gain counters. These cars disfigure the streets,
but no one has made serious protest, for are
not the Hoosiers welcome to their capital, no
matter how or when they visit it; and is not
this free intercourse, as the phrase has it, "a
good thing for Indianapolis"? This contact
between town and country tends to stimulate
a state feeling, and as the capital grows this
intimacy will have an increasing value.

There is something neighborly and cozy
about Indianapolis. The man across the street
or next door will share any good thing he has
with you, whether it be a cure for rheumatism,
a new book, or the garden hose. It is a town
where doing as one likes is not a mere possibil-
ity, but an inherent right. The woman of Indianapolis is not afraid to venture abroad with
her market-basket, albeit she may carry it in
an automobile. The public market at Indianapolis is an ancient and honorable institution,
and there is no shame but much honor in being
seen there in conversation with the farmer
and the gardener or the seller of herbs, in the
early hours of the morning. The market is so
thoroughly established in public affection that

A Provincial Capital

the society reporter walks its aisles in pursuit
of news. The true Indianapolis housewife goes
to market; the mere resident of the city orders
by telephone, and meekly accepts what the
grocer has to offer; and herein lies a difference that is not half so superficial as it may
sound, for at heart the people who are related
to the history and tradition of Indianapolis
are simple and frugal, and if they read Emerson
and Browning by the evening lamp, they know
no reason why they should not distinguish,
the next morning, between the yellow-legged
chicken offered by the farmer's wife at the
market and frozen fowls of doubtful authenticity
that have been held for a season in cold storage.

The narrow margin between the great parties in Indiana has made the capital a centre of
incessant political activity. The geographical
position of the city has also contributed to this,
the state leaders and managers being constant
visitors. Every second man you meet is a
statesman; every third man is an orator. The
largest social club in Indiana exacts a promise
of fidelity to the Republican party, — or did,
until insurgency made the close scrutiny of the

73

members' partisanship impolite if not impolitic!—and within its portals chances and changes of men and measures are discussed tirelessly. And the pilgrim is not bored with local affairs; not a bit of it! Municipal dangers do not trouble the Indianapolitan; his eye is on the White House, not the town hall. The presence in the city through many years of men of national prominence—Morton, Harrison, Hendricks, McDonald, English, Gresham, Turpie, of the old order, and Fairbanks, Kern, Beveridge, and Marshall in recent years—has kept Indianapolis to the fore as a political centre. Geography is an important factor in the distribution of favors by state conventions. Rivalry between the smaller towns is not so marked as their united stand against the capital, though this feeling seems to be abating. The city has had, at least twice, both United States Senators; but governors have usually been summoned from the country. Harrison was defeated for governor by a farmer (1876), in a heated campaign, in which "Kid-Gloved Harrison" was held up to derision by the adherents of "Blue-Jeans Will-

A Provincial Capital

iams." And again, in 1880, a similar situation
was presented in the contest for the same office
between Albert G. Porter and Franklin Landers, both of Indianapolis, though Landers stood
ruggedly for the "blue jeans" idea.

The high tide of political interest was
reached in the summer and fall of 1888, when
Harrison made his campaign for the presidency,
largely from his own doorstep. Marion County,
of which Indianapolis is the seat, was for many
years Republican; but neither county nor city
has lately been "safely" Democratic or Republican. At the city election held in October,
1904, a Democrat was elected mayor over a
Republican candidate who had been renomi-
nated in a "snap" convention, in the face of
aggressive opposition within his party. The
issue was tautly drawn between corruption
and vice on the one hand and law and order
on the other. An independent candidate, who
had also the Prohibition support, received
over five thousand votes.

The difficulties in the way of securing intelligent and honest city government have,
however, multiplied with the growth of the

A Provincial Capital

city. The American municipal problem is
as acutely presented in Indianapolis as elsewhere. The more prosperous a city the less
time have the beneficiaries of its prosperity for
self-government. It is much simpler to allow
politicians of gross incapacity and leagued with
vice to levy taxes and expend the income according to the devices and desires of their own
hearts and pockets than to find reputable and
patriotic citizens to administer the business.
Here as elsewhere the party system is indubitably at the root of the evil. It happens, indeed,
that Indianapolis is even more the victim of
partisanship than other cities of approxim-
ately the same size for the reason that both
the old political organizations feel that the loss
of the city at a municipal election jeopardizes
the chances of success in general elections.
Just what effect the tariff and other national
issues have upon street cleaning and the polic-
ing of a city has never been explained. It is
interesting to note that the park board, whose
members serve without pay, has been, since
the adoption of the city charter, a commission
of high intelligence and unassailable integrity.

A Provincial Capital

The standard having been so established no mayor is likely soon to venture to consign this board's important and responsible functions to the common type of city hall hangers-on.

It is one of the most maddening of the anomalies of American life that municipal pride should exhaust its energy in the exploitation of factory sites and the strident advertisement of the number of freight cars handled in railroad yards, while the municipal corporation itself is turned over to any band of charlatans and buccaneers that may seek to capture it. In 1911–12 the municipal government had reached the lowest ebb in the city's history. It had become so preposterous and improvement was so imperatively demanded that many citizens, both as individuals and in organizations, began to interest themselves in plans for reform. The hope here as elsewhere seems to be in the young men, particularly of the college type, who find in local government a fine exercise for their talents and zeal.

In this connection it may be said that the Indianapolis public schools owe their marked excellence and efficiency to their complete di-

A Provincial Capital

vorcement from political influence. This has not only assured the public an intelligent and honest expenditure of school funds, but it has created a corps spirit among the city's teachers, admirable in itself, and tending to cumulative benefits not yet realized. The superintendent of schools has absolute power of appointment, and he is accountable only to the commissioners, and they in turn are entirely independent of the mayor and other city officers. Positions on the school board are not sought by politicians. The incumbents serve without pay, and the public evince a disposition to find good men and to keep them in office.

The soldiers' monument at Indianapolis is a testimony to the deep impression made by the Civil War on the people of the State. The monument is to Indianapolis what the Washington Monument is to the national capital. The incoming traveler beholds it afar, and within the city it is almost an inescapable thing, though with the advent of the skyscraper it is rapidly losing its fine dignity as the chief incident of the skyline. It stands in a circular plaza that was originally a park known

A Provincial Capital

as the "Governor's Circle." This was long ago abandoned as a site for the governor's mansion, but it offered an ideal spot for a monument to Indiana soldiers, when, in 1887, the General Assembly authorized its construction. The height of the monument from the street level is two hundred and eighty-four feet and it stands on a stone terrace one hundred and ten feet in diameter. The shaft is crowned by a statue of Victory thirty-eight feet high. It is built throughout of Indiana limestone. The fountains at the base, the heroic sculptured groups "War" and "Peace," and the bronze astragals representing the army and navy, are admirable in design and execution. The whole effect is one of poetic beauty and power. There is nothing cheap, tawdry, or commonplace in this magnificent tribute of Indiana to her soldiers. The monument is a memorial of the soldiers of all the wars in which Indiana has participated. The veterans of the Civil War protested against this, and the controversy was long and bitter; but the capture of Vincennes from the British in 1779 is made to link Indiana to the war of the Revolution; and the

battle of Tippecanoe, to the war of 1812. The
war with Mexico, and seven thousand four
hundred men enlisted for the Spanish War are
likewise remembered. It is, however, the war
of the Rebellion, whose effect on the social and
political life of Indiana was so tremendous,
that gives the monument its great cause for
being. The white male population of Indiana
in 1860 was 693,348; the total enlistment of
soldiers during the ensuing years of war was
210,497! The names of these men lie safe for
posterity in the base of the gray shaft.

The newspaper paragrapher has in recent
years amused himself at the expense of Indiana as a literary centre, but Indianapolis as a
village boasted writers of at least local reputation, and Coggeshall's "Poets and Poetry
of the West" (1867) attributes half a dozen
poets to the Hoosier capital. The Indianapolis
press has from the beginning been distinguished
by enterprise and decency, and in several instances by vigorous independence. The literary
quality of the city's newspapers was high, even
in the early days, and the standard has not been
lowered. Poets with cloaks and canes were, in

A Provincial Capital

the eighties, pretty prevalent in Market Street
near the post-office, the habitat then of most
of the newspapers. The poets read their verses
to one another and cursed the magazines. A
reporter for one of the papers, who had scored
the triumph of a poem in the "Atlantic," was
a man of mark among the guild for years. The
local wits stabbed the fledgeling bards with
their gentle ironies. A young woman of social
prominence printed some verses in an Indianapolis newspaper, and one of her acquaintances, when asked for his opinion of them,
said they were creditable and ought to be set
to music — and played as an instrumental
piece! The wide popularity attained by Mr.
James Whitcomb Riley quickened the literary
impulse, and the fame of his elders and pre-
decessors suffered severely from the fact that
he did not belong to the cloaked brigade.
General Lew Wallace never lived at Indianapolis save for a few years in boyhood, while
his father was governor, though toward the
end of his life he spent his winters there.
Maurice Thompson's muse scorned "paven
ground," and he was little known at the capital

even during his term of office as state geologist, when he came to town frequently from his home in Crawfordsville. Mr. Booth Tarkington, the most cosmopolitan of Hoosiers, has lifted the banner anew for a younger generation through his successful essays in fiction and the drama.

If you do not in this provincial capital meet an author at every corner, you are at least never safe from men and women who read books. In many Missouri River towns a stranger must still listen to the old wail against the railroads; at Indianapolis he must listen to politics, and possibly some one will ask his opinion of a sonnet, just as though it were a cigar. A judge of the United States Court sitting at Indianapolis, was in the habit of locking the door of his private office and reading Horace to visiting attorneys. There was, indeed, a time — *consule Planco* — when most of the federal officeholders at Indianapolis were bookish men. Three successive clerks of the federal courts were scholars; the pension agent was an enthusiastic Shakespearean; the district attorney was a poet; and the master of chancery a man of varied learning, who was so excellent a talker

82

A Provincial Capital

that, when he met Lord Chief Justice Coleridge abroad, the English jurist took the Hoosier with him on circuit, and wrote to the justice of the American Supreme Court who had introduced them, to "send me another man as good."

It is possible for a community which may otherwise lack a true local spirit to be unified through the possession of a sense of humor; and even in periods of financial depression the town has always enjoyed the saving grace of a cheerful, centralized intelligence. The first tavern philosophers stood for this, and the courts of the early times were enlivened by it, — as witness all Western chronicles. The Middle Western people are preëminently humorous, particularly those of the Southern strain from which Lincoln sprang. During all the years that the Hoosier suffered the reproach of the outside world, the citizen of the capital never failed to appreciate the joke when it was on himself; and looking forth from the wicket of the city gate, he was still more keenly appreciative when it was "on" his neighbors. The Hoosier is a natural story-teller; he relishes a joke, and to

A Provincial Capital

talk is his ideal of social enjoyment. This was true of the early Hoosier, and it is true to-day of his successor at the capital. The Monday night meetings of the Indianapolis Literary Club — organized in 1877 and with a continuous existence to this time — have been marked by racy talk. The original members are nearly all gone; but the sayings of a group of them — the stiletto thrusts of Fishback, the lawyer; the droll inadvertences of Livingston Howland, the judge; and the inimitable anecdotes of Myron Reed, soldier and preacher — crept beyond the club's walls and became town property. This club is old and well seasoned. It is exclusive — so much so that one of its luminaries remarked that if all of its members should be expelled for any reason, none could hope to be readmitted. It has entertained but four pilgrims from the outer world, — Matthew Arnold, Dean Farrar, Joseph Parker, and John Fiske.

The Hoosier capital has always been susceptible to the charms of oratory. Most of the great lecturers in the golden age of the American lyceum were welcomed cordially at Indianapolis. The Indianapolis pulpit has been served

A Provincial Capital

by many able men, and great store is still set by preaching. When Henry Ward Beecher ministered to the congregation of the Second Presbyterian Church (1838–46), his superior talents were recognized and appreciated. He gave a series of seven lectures to the young men of the city during the winter of 1843–44, on such subjects as "Industry," "Gamblers and Gambling," "Popular Amusements," etc., which were published at Indianapolis immediately, in response to an urgent request signed by thirteen prominent citizens.

The women of Indianapolis have aided greatly in fashioning the city into an enlightened community. The wives and daughters of the founders were often women of cultivation, and much in the character of the city to-day is plainly traceable to their work and example. During the Civil War they did valiant service in caring for the Indiana soldier. They built for themselves in 1888 a building — the Propylæum — where many clubs meet; and they were long the mainstay of the Indianapolis Art Association, which, by a generous and unexpected bequest a few years ago, now boasts a perma-

A Provincial Capital

nent museum and school. It is worth remembering that the first woman's club — in the West, at least — was organized on Hoosier soil — at Robert Owen's New Harmony — in 1859. The women of the Hoosier capital have addressed themselves zealously in many organizations to the study of all subjects related to good government. The apathy bred of commercial success that has dulled the civic consciousness of their fathers and husbands and brothers has had the effect of stimulating their curiosity and quickening their energies along lines of political and social development.

I have been retouching here and there this paper as it was written ten years ago. In the intervening decade the population of Indianapolis has increased 38.1 per cent, jumping from 169,161 to 233,650, and passing both Providence and Louisville. Something of the Southern languor that once seemed so charming — something of what the plodding citizens of the mule-car days liked to call "atmosphere" — has passed. And yet the changes are, after all, chiefly such as address the eye rather than the spirit. There are more people, but there are more good people! The coming of the army post has widened our political and social horizons. The building of the Homeric speedway that has caused us to be written large on the world's pink sporting pages, and the invasion of foreigners, have not seriously disturbed the old neighborliness, kindliness, and homely cheer. Elsewhere in these pages I mention the passing of the church as the bulwark behind which this community had intrenched itself; and yet much the same spirituality that was once observable endures, though known by new names.

The old virtues must still be dominant, for visitors sensitive to such impressions seem to be conscious of their existence. Only to-day Mr. Arnold Bennett, discoursing of America in "Harper's Magazine," finds here exactly the things whose passing it is the local fashion to deplore. In our maple-lined streets he was struck by the number of detached houses, each with its own garden. He found in these homes "the expression of a race incapable of looking foolish, of being giddy, of running to extremes." And I am cheered by his declaration of a belief

87

A Provincial Capital

that in some of the comfortable parlors of our quiet thoroughfares there are "minor millionaires who wonder whether, outsoaring the ambition of a bit of property, they would be justified in creeping downtown and buying a cheap automobile!" And I had been afraid that every man among us with anything tangible enough to mortgage had undertaken the task of advertising one of our chief industries by modernizing Ezekiel's vision of the wheels!

It is cheering to know that this pilgrim from the Five Towns thought us worthy of a place in his odyssey, and that his snapshots reveal so much of what my accustomed eyes sometimes fail to see. I am glad to be reëstablished by so penetrating an observer in my old faith that there are planted here on the West Fork of White River some of the roots of "essential America." If we are not typical Americans we offer the nearest approach to it that I, in my incurable provincialism, know where to lay hands on.

Experience and the Calendar

Experience and the Calendar

USELESS, quite useless, young man," said
the doctor, pursing his lips; and as he has
a nice feeling for climax, he slapped the reins on
Dobbin's broad back and placidly drove away.

Beneath that flapping gray hat his wrinkled
face was unusually severe. His eyes really
seemed to flash resentment through his green
spectacles. The doctor's remark related to my
manipulation of a new rose-sprayer which I had
purchased this morning at the village hardware
store, and was directing against the pests on
my crimson ramblers when he paused to tell me
that he had tried that identical device last year
and found it worthless. As his shabby old phae-
ton rounded the corner, I turned the sprayer
over to my young undergraduate friend Septimus, and hurried in to set down a few truths
about the doctor.

He is, as you may already have guessed, the
venerable Doctor Experience, of the well-
known university that bears his name. He is

Experience and the Calendar

a person of quality and distinction, and the most quoted of all the authorities on life and conduct. How empty the day would be in which we did not hear some one say, "Experience has taught me —" In the University of Experience the Doctor fills all the chairs; and all his utterances, one may say, are *ex cathedra*.

He is as respectable for purposes of quotation as Thomas à Kempis or Benjamin Franklin. We really imagine — we who are alumni of the old doctor's ivy-mantled knowledge-house, and who recall the austerity of his curriculum and the frugality of Sunday evening tea at his table — that his own courses were immensely profitable to us. We remember well how he warned us against yielding to the persuasions of the world, the flesh, and the devil, illustrating his points with anecdotes from his own long and honorable career. He used to weep over us, too, in a fashion somewhat dispiriting; but we loved him, and sometimes as we sit in the winter twilight thinking of the days that are no more, we recall him in a mood of affection and regret, and do not mind at all that cheerless motto in the seal of the university corporation, "*Experientia*

Experience and the Calendar

docet stultos," to which he invariably calls attention after morning prayers.

"My young friends," he says, "I hope and trust that my words may be the means of saving you from much of the heartache and sorrow of this world. When I was young —"

This phrase is the widely accepted signal for shuffling the feet and looking bored. We turn away from the benign doctor at his reading-desk, fumbling at that oft-repeated lecture which our fathers and grandfathers remember and quote, — we turn our gaze to the open windows and the sunlight. The philosophy of life is in process of making out there, — a new philosophy for every hour, with infinite spirit and color, and anon we hear bugles crying across the hills of our dreams. "When I was young!" If we were not the politest imaginable body of students, — we who take Doctor Experience's course because it is (I blush at the confession) a "snap," — we should all be out of the window and over the hills and far away.

The great weakness of Experience as a teacher lies in the fact that truth is so alterable. We have hardly realized how utterly the snows

Experience and the Calendar

and roses of yesteryear vanish before the amiable book agent points out to us the obsolete character of our most prized encyclopædia. All books should be purchased with a view to their utility in lifting the baby's chin a proper distance above the breakfast table; for, quite likely, this will soon become their sole office in the household. Within a fifteen-minute walk of the window by which I write lives a man who rejects utterly the idea that the world is round, and he is by no means a fool. He is a far more interesting person, I dare say, than Copernicus or Galileo ever was; and his strawberries are the earliest and the best produced in our township. Truth, let us say, is a continuing matter, and hope springeth eternal. This is where I parted company with the revered doctor long ago. His inability to catch bass in the creek isn't going to keep me at home to-morrow morning. For all I care, he may sit on his veranda and talk himself hoarse to his old friend, Professor Killjoy, whose gum shoes and ear-muffs are a feature of our village landscape.

When you and I, my brother, are called on to address the young, how blithely we congratu-

Experience and the Calendar

late our hearers upon being the inheritors of the wisdom of all the ages. This is one of the greatest of fallacies. The twentieth century dawned upon American States that were bored by the very thought of the Constitution, and willing to forget that venerable document at least long enough to experiment with the Initiative, the Referendum, and the Recall. What some Lord Chief Justice announced as sound law a hundred years ago means nothing to commonwealths that have risen since the motor-car began honking in the highway. On a starry night in the spring of 1912 a veteran sea-captain, with wireless warnings buttoned under his pea-jacket, sent the finest ship in the world smashing into an iceberg. All the safety devices known to railroading cannot prevent some engineer from occasionally trying the experiment of running two trains on a single track. With the full weight of the experience of a thousand years against him the teller begins to transfer the bank's money to his own pocket, knowing well the hazard and the penalty.

We pretend to invoke dear old Experience as though he were a god, fondly imagining that an

Experience and the Calendar

honest impulse demands that we appeal to him
as an arbiter. But when we have submitted our
case and listened to his verdict, we express our
thanks and go away and do exactly as we please.
We all carry our troubles to the friends whose
sympathy we know outweighs their wisdom.
We want them to pat us on the back and tell
us that we are doing exactly right. If by any
chance they are bold enough to give us an
honest judgment based on real convictions, we
depart with a grievance, our confidence shaken.
We lean upon our friends, to be sure; but we
rely upon them to bail us out after the forts of
folly have crashed about our ears and we pine
in the donjon, rather than on their advice that
might possibly have preserved us on the right
side of the barricade. And I may note here,
that of all the offices that man may undertake,
that of the frank friend is the most thankless.
The frank friend! It is he who told you yesterday that you were looking wretchedly ill. Doctor Experience had warned *him;* and he felt
it to be his duty to stop *you* in your headlong
plunge. To-morrow he will drop in to tell you
in gentle terms that your latest poem is —

Experience and the Calendar

well, he hates to say it — but he fears it is n't up to your old mark! The frank friend, you may remember, is Doctor Experience's favorite pupil.

We are all trying to square wisdom with our own aims and errors. Professional men, whose business is the giving of advice, are fully aware of this. Death is the only arbiter who can enforce his own writs, and it is not for man to speak a final word on any matter.

I was brought up to have an immense respect — reverence, even — for law. It seemed to me in my youth to embody a tremendous philosophy. Here, I used to say, as I pondered opinion and precedent, — here is the very flower and fruit of the wisdom of the ages. I little dreamed that both sides of every case may be supported by authorities of equal dignity. Imagine my bewilderment when I found that a case which is likely to prove weak before one infallible judge may be shifted with little trouble to another, equally infallible, but with views known to be friendly to the cause in question. I sojourned for a time in a judicial circuit where there was considerable traveling

Experience and the Calendar

to be done by the court and bar. The lawyer who was most enterprising in securing a sleeping-car stateroom wherein to play poker — discreetly and not too successfully — with the judge, was commonly supposed to have the best chance of winning his cases.

Our neighbors' failures are really of no use to us. "No Admittance" and "Paint" are not accepted by the curious world as warnings, but as invitations.

> "A sign once caught the casual eye,
>   And it said, 'Paint';
> And every one who passed it by,
>   Sinner or saint,
> Into the fresh green color must
>   Make it his biz
> A doubting finger-point to thrust,
> That he, accepting naught on trust,
>   Might say, 'It is, it is!'"

Cynic, do I hear? The term is not one of opprobrium. A cynic is the alert and discerning man who declines to cut the cotton-filled pie or pick up the decoy purse on All Fools' Day.

We are bound to test for ourselves the identical heating apparatus which the man next door cast away as rubbish last spring. We know

Experience and the Calendar

why its heat units were unsatisfactory to him,
— it was because his chimneys were too small;
and though our own are as like them as two
peas we proceed to our own experiment with
our eyes wide open. Mrs. B telephones to Mrs.
A and asks touching the merits, habits, and pre-
vious condition of servitude of the cook Mrs. A
discharged this morning. Mrs. A, who holds an
honorary degree bestowed upon her by the good
Doctor Experience, leans upon the telephone
and explains with conscientious detail the de-
ficiencies of Mary Ann. She does as she would
be done by and does it thoroughly. But what is
her astonishment to learn the next day that
Mary Ann's trunk has been transferred to Mrs.
B's third story; that Mary Ann's impossible
bread and deadly cake are upon Mrs. B's table!
Mrs. B, too, took a course of lectures under
Doctor Experience, and she admires him
greatly; but what do these facts avail her when
guests are alighting at the door and Mary Ann
is the only cook visible in the urban landscape? Moreover, Mrs. A *always was* (delectable colloquialism!) a hard mistress, and
Mrs. B must, she feels, judge of these matters

99

for herself. And so — so — say we all of us!

Men who have done post-graduate work in the good doctor's school are no better fortified against error than the rest of us who may never have got beyond his kindergarten. The results might be different if it were not that Mistress Vanity by her arts and graces demoralizes the doctor's students, whose eyes wander to the windows as she flits across the campus. Conservative bankers, sage lawyers, and wise legislators have been the frequent and easy prey of the gold-brick operator. The police announce a new crop of "suckers" every spring, — which seems to indicate that Mistress Vanity wields a greater influence than Doctor Experience. These words stare at me oddly in type; they are the symbols of a disagreeable truth, — and yet we may as well face it. The eternal ego will not bow to any dingy doctor whose lectures only illustrate his own inability to get on in the world.

The best skating is always on thin ice, — we like to feel it crack and yield under our feet; there is a deadly fascination in the thought of the twenty or forty feet of cold water beneath. Last year's mortality list cuts (dare I do it?) no ice with us; we must make our own experiments, while the doctor screams himself hoarse from his bonfire on the bank. He has held many an inquest on this darkling shore of the river of time, and he will undoubtedly live to hold many another; but thus far we have not been the subjects; and when it comes to the mistakes of others we are all delighted to serve on the coroner's jury.

It is n't well for us to be saved from too many blunders; we need the discipline of failure. It is better to fail than never to try, and the man who can contemplate the graveyard of his own hopes without bitterness will not always be ignored by the gods of success.

Septimus had a narrow escape yesterday. He was reading "Tom Jones" in the college library, when the doctor stole close behind him and Septimus's nervous system experienced a terrible shock. But it was the doctor's opportunity. "Read biography, young man; biographies of the good and great are veritable textbooks in this school!" So you may observe

Experience and the Calendar

Septimus to-day sprawled under the noblest elm on the campus, with his eyes bulging out as he follows Napoleon on the retreat from Russia. He has firmly resolved to profit by the failure of "the darkly-gifted Corsican." To-morrow evening, when he tries to hitch the doctor's good old Dobbin to the chapel bell, and falls from the belfry into the arms of the village constable, he is far more tolerant of Napoleon's mistakes. An interesting biography is no more valuable than a good novel. If life were an agreed state of facts and not a joyful experiment, then we might lean upon biography as final; but in this and in all matters, let us deal squarely with Youth. Boswell's "Johnson" is only gossip raised to the highest power; the reading of it will make Septimus cheerfuler, but it will not keep him from wearing a dinner coat to a five o'clock tea or teach him how to earn more than four dollars a week.

We have brought existence to an ideal state when at every breakfast table we face a new world with no more use for yesterday than for the grounds of yesterday's coffee. The wisdom behind us is a high wall which we cannot scale if

Experience and the Calendar

we would. Its very height is tempting, but there is no rose-garden beyond it — only a bleak plain with the sea of time gnawing its dreary shores.

To be old and to know ten thousand things — there is something august and majestic in the thought; but to be young and ignorant, to see yesterday pass, a shining ripple on the flood of oblivion, and then to buckle down to the day's business, — there's a better thing than being old and wise! We are forever praising the unconscious ease of great literature; and that ease — typical of the life and time reflected — was a thing of the day, with no yesterdays' dead weight dragging it down. Whitman's charm for those of us who like him lies in the fact that he does n't invite us to a rummage sale of cast-off raiment, but offers fabrics that are fresh and in new patterns. We have all known that same impatience of the past that he voices so stridently. The world is as new to him as it was to Isaiah or Homer.

"When I heard the learned astronomer,
When the proofs and figures were ranged in columns
    before me,

Experience and the Calendar

When I was shown the charts and diagrams, to add,
    divide, and measure them;
When I, sitting, heard the astronomer where he lec-
    tured with much applause in the lecture room,
How soon, unaccountably, I became tired and sick,
Till rising and gliding out I wander'd off by myself,
In the mystical moist night-air, and from time to time
Look'd up in perfect silence at the stars."

The old doctor can name all the stars without a telescope, but he does not know that in
joy they "perform their shining." The real
note in life is experiment and quest, and we
are detached far more than we realize from
what was and concerned with what is and
may be.

There is a delightful comedy, — long popular
in England and known in America, in which a
Martian appears on earth to teach Dickens-like
lessons of unselfishness to men. Since witness-
ing it, I have often indulged in speculations as
to the sensations of a pilgrim who might wing
his way from another star to this earth, losing in
the transition all knowledge of his own past
— and come freshly upon our world and its
achievements, beholding man at his best and
worst without any knowledge whatever of our

104

Experience and the Calendar

history or of the evolution through which we have become what we are. There you would have a critic who could view our world with fresh eyes. What we were yesterday would mean nothing to him, and what we are to-day he might judge honestly from a standpoint of utility or beauty. Not what was old or new, but what was good, would interest him — not whether our morals are better than those of our ancestors, but whether they are of any use at all. The croaking plaint of Not-What-It-Used-To-Be, the sanguine It-Will-Come-In-Time, would have no meaning for such a judge.

"And not only so, but we glory in tribulations also; knowing that tribulation worketh patience; and patience, experience; and experience, hope."

The conjunction of these last words is happy. Verily in experience lies our hope. In learning what to do and what not to do, in stumbling, falling to rise again and faring ever upward and onward. Yes, in and through experience lies our hope, but not, O brother, a wisdom gained vicariously, — not yours for me nor mine for

Experience and the Calendar

you, — nor from enduring books, charm they
never so wisely, — but every one of us, old and
young, for himself.

Literature is rich in advice that is utterly
worthless. Life's "Book of Don'ts" is only read
for the footnotes that explain why particular
"don'ts" failed, — it has become in reality the
"Book of Don'ts that Did." It is pleasant to
remember that the gentle Autocrat, a man of
science as well as of letters, did not allow professional courtesy to stand in the way of a characteristic fling at Doctor Experience. He goes,
in his contempt, to the stupid creatures of the
barnyard, and points in high disdain to "that
solemn fowl, Experience, who, according to my
observation, cackles oftener than she drops real
live eggs."

If the old doctor were to be taken at his own
valuation and we should be disposed to profit
by his teachings, our lives would be a dreary
round; and youth, particularly, would find the
ginger savorless in the jar and the ale stale in
the pot. I saw my venerable friend walking
abroad the other day in the flowered dressing-
gown which he so much affects, wearing his

Experience and the Calendar

familiar classroom smile. I heard him warning a boy, who was hammering a boat together out of wretchedly flimsy material, that his argosy would never float; but the next day I saw the young Columbus faring forth, with his coat for sail, and saw him turn the bend in the creek safely and steer beyond "the gray Azores" of his dreams.

The young admiral cannot escape the perils of the deep, and like St. Paul he will know shipwreck before his marine career is ended; but why discourage him? Not the doctor's hapless adventures, but the lad's own are going to make a man of him. I know a town where, thirty years ago, an afternoon newspaper failed about once every six months. There was, so the wiseacres affirmed, no manner of use in trying it again. But a tow-headed boy put his small patrimony into a venture, reinforced it with vigorous independence and integrity, and made it a source of profit to himself and a valued agent in the community. In twenty years the property sold for a million dollars. Greatness, I assure Septimus, consists in achieving the impossible.

Experience and the Calendar

"Daughters of Time, the hypocritic Days,
  Muffled and dumb like barefoot dervishes,
  And marching single in an endless file,
  Bring diadems and fagots in their hands.
  To each they offer gifts after his will,
  Bread, kingdoms, stars, and sky that holds them
    all.
  I, in my pleachèd garden, watched the pomp,
  Forgot my morning wishes, hastily
  Took a few herbs and apples, and the Day
  Turned and departed silent. I, too late,
  Under her solemn fillet saw the scorn."

The season is at hand when Time throws his annual challenge in our teeth. The bell tinkles peremptorily and a calendar is thrust upon us. November is still young when we are dragged upon the threshold of another year. The leisurely dismissal of the old year is no longer possible; we may indulge in no lingering good-bye, but the old fellow hustles out in haste, with apologetic, shrinking step and we slam the door upon him. It is off with the old love and on with the new, whether we will or no. I solemnly protest against the invasion of the calendar. In an age that boasts of freedom, I rebel against a tyrant who comes merely to warn us of the fugitive character of Time; for that sharp elbow

108

Experience and the Calendar

in the ribs has prodded many a noble soul to his
death. These pretty devices that we are asked
to hang upon our walls are the seductive advertisements of an insinuating and implacable foe.
We are asked to be *particeps criminis* in his
hideous trade, for must I not tear off and cast
as rubbish to the void a day, a week, a month,
that I may not have done with at all? Why,
may I ask, should I throw my yesterdays into
the waste-basket? Yet if I fail, falling only a
few leaves behind, is not my shameless inef-
ficiency and heedlessness paraded before the
world? How often have I delivered myself up
to my enemies by suffering April to laugh her
girlish laughter through torrid July? I know
well the insinuating smile of the friend who,
dropping in on a peaceful morning, when Time,
as far as I am concerned, has paused in the hay-
field to dream upon his scythe handle, walks
coolly to the calendar and brings me up to date
with a fine air of rebuke, as though he were
conferring the greatest favor in the world. I am
sure that I should have no standing with my
neighbors if they knew that I rarely wind my
watch and that the clocks in my house, save

Experience and the Calendar

one or two that are kept going merely to
avoid explanations, are never wound.

There is a gentle irony in the fact that the
most insolent dispensers of calendars are the
life insurance companies. It is a legitimate part
of their nefarious game: you and I are their
natural prey, and if they can accent for us the
mortality of the flesh by holding up before us,
in compact form, the slight round of the year,
they are doing much to impress upon us the
appalling brevity of our most reasonable ex-
pectancy. How weak we are to suffer the in-
timidation of these soulless corporations, who
thrust their wares upon us as much as to say,
"Here's a new year, and you'd better make
the most of it, for there's no saying when you
will get another." You, my friend, with your
combined calendar and memorandum always
before you, may pledge all your to-morrows if
you will; but as for me the Hypocritic Days,
the Barefoot Dervishes, may ring my bell until
they exhaust the battery without gaining a
single hour as my grudging alms.

We are all prone to be cowards, and to bend
before the tyrant whose banner is spread vic-

Experience and the Calendar

toriously on all our walls. Poets and philosophers aid and abet him; the preachers are forever telling us what a dreadful fellow he is, and warning us that if we don't get on the good side of him we are lost forever, — mere wreckage on a grim, inhospitable shore. Hypocrisy and false oaths are born of such teaching. Januarius, let us remember, was two-faced, and it has come about naturally that New Year's oaths carry a reserve. They are not, in fact, serious obligations. It is a poor soul that sets apart a certain number of days for rectitude, and I can't for the life of me see anything noble in making a constable of the calendar. I find with joy that I am freeing myself of the tyrant's thrall. I am never quite sure of the day of the week; I date my letters yesterday or to-morrow with equal indifference. June usually thrusts her roses into my windows before I change the year in dating my letters. The magazines seem leagued with the calendar for man's undoing. I sometimes rush home from an inspection of a magazine counter in mad haste to get where Oblivion cannot stretch forth a long, lean arm and pluck me into the eternal shades; for I

Experience and the Calendar

decline with all the strength of my crude Western nature, to countenance the manufacture of yesterdays, no matter how cheerful they may be, out of my confident to-morrows. A March magazine flung into the teeth of a February blizzard does not fool the daffodils a particle. This stamping of months that have not arrived upon our current literature is nothing more or less than counterfeiting; — or rather, the issuing of false currency by the old Tyrant who stands behind the counter of the Bank of Time. And there is the railway time-table, — the unconscious comic utterance of the *Zeitgeist!* If the 12.59 is one minute or one hour late, who cares, I wonder? Who am I, pray, that I should stuff my pocket with calendars and time-tables? Why not throw the charts to the fishes and let the winds have their will with us awhile! Let us, I beg, leave some little margin in our lives for the shock of surprise!

The Daughters of Time are charming young persons, and they may offer me all the bread, kingdoms, stars they like; but they must cheer up or keep out of my front yard! No shuffling around, like Barefoot Dervishes; but in golden

Experience and the Calendar

sandals let them come, and I will kindle a fire of next year's calendars in their honor. When the snows weigh heavily upon the hills, let us not mourn for yesterday or waste time in idle speculations at the fireside, but address ourselves manfully to the hour's business. And as some of the phrases of Horace's ode to Thaliarchus rap for attention in an old file box at the back of my head, I set down a pleasant rendering of them by Mr. Charles Edmund Merrill, Jr.

> "To-morrow? Shall the fleeting years
>   Abide our questioning? They go
> All heedless of our hopes and fears.
> To-morrow? 'T is not ours to know
>   That we again shall see the flowers.
> To-morrow is the gods', but oh,
>   To-day is ours."

We all salute heartily and sincerely the "grandeur and exquisiteness" of old age. It is not because Doctor Experience is old that we distrust his judgment; it is not his judgment that we distrust half so much as his facts. They are good, as facts go, but we are all foreordained and predestined to reap our own crop. He need not take the trouble to nail his sign, "No

Experience and the Calendar

thoroughfare," on the highways that have perplexed him, for we, too, must stray into the brambles and stumble at the ford. It is decreed that we sail without those old charts of his, and we drop our signal-books and barometer overboard without a qualm. The reefs change with every tide, adding zest to our adventure; and while the gulfs may wash us down, there's always the chance that, in our own way and after much anxious and stupid sailing, we may ground our barnacled hulks on the golden sands of the Happy Isles. Our blood cries for the open sea or the long white road, and

"Rare the moment and exceeding fleet
  When the spring sunlight, tremulous and thin,
Makes glad the pulses with tumultuous beat
  For meadows never won nor wandered in."

Should Smith go to Church?

Should Smith go to Church?

I THINK he should. Moreover, I think I should set Smith an example by placing myself on Sunday morning in a pew from which he may observe me at my devotions. Smith and I attended the same Sunday school when we were boys, and remained for church afterwards as a matter of course. Smith now spends his Sunday mornings golfing, or pottering about his garden, or in his club or office, and after the midday meal he takes a nap and loads his family into a motor for a flight countryward. It must be understood that I do not offer myself as a pattern for Smith. While I resent being classified with the lost sheep, I am, nevertheless, a restless member of the flock, prone to leap the wall and wander. Smith is the best of fellows, — an average twentieth-century American, diligent in business, a kind husband and father, and in politics anxious to vote for what he believes to be the best interests of the country.

Should Smith go to Church?

In the community where we were reared it was not respectable not to go to church. I remember distinctly that in my boyhood people who were not affiliated with some church were looked upon as lawless pariahs. An infidel was a marked man: one used to be visible in the streets I frequented, and I never passed him without a thrill of horror. Our city was long known as "a poor theatre town," where only Booth in *Hamlet* and Jefferson in *Rip* might be patronized by church-going people who valued their reputations. Yet in the same community no reproach attaches to-day to the non-church-going citizen. A majority of the men I know best, in cities large and small, do not go to church. Most of them are in nowise antagonistic to religion; they are merely indifferent. Clearly, there must be some reason for this change. It is inconceivable that men would lightly put from them the faith of their fathers through which they are promised redemption from sin and everlasting life.

Now and then I hear it asserted that the church is not losing its hold upon the people. Many clergymen and laymen resent the oft-

Should Smith go to Church?

repeated statement that we Americans are not as deeply swayed by religion as in other times; but this seems to me a case of whistling through a graveyard on a dark night.

A recent essayist,[1] writing defensively of the church, cries, in effect, that it is moving toward the light; don't shoot! He declares that no one who has not contributed something toward the solution of the church's problem has earned the right to criticize. I am unable to sympathize with this reasoning. The church is either the repository of the Christian religion on earth, the divinely inspired and blessed tabernacle of the faith of Christ, or it is a stupendous fraud. There is no sound reason why the church should not be required to give an account of its stewardship. If it no longer attracts men and women in our strenuous and impatient America, then it is manifestly unjust to deny to outsiders the right of criticism. Smith is far from being a fool, and if by his test of "What's in it for me?" he finds the church wanting, it is, as he would say, "up to the church" to expend

[1] "Heckling the Church," *The Atlantic Monthly*, December, 1911.

some of its energy in proving that there is a good deal in it for him. It is unfair to say to Smith, who has utterly lost touch with the church, that before he is qualified to criticize the ways and the manners of churches he must renew an allegiance which he was far too intelligent and conscientious to sever without cause.

Nor can I justly be denied the right of criticism because my own ardor is diminished, and I am frequently conscious of a distinct lukewarmness. I confess to a persistent need in my own life for the support, the stimulus, the hope, that is inherent in the teachings of Christianity; nevertheless the church — that is to say, the Protestantism with which I am familiar — has seemed to me increasingly a wholly inadequate medium for communicating to men such as Smith and myself the help and inspiration of the vision of Christ. There are far too many Smiths who do not care particularly whether the churches prosper or die. And I urge that Smith is worthy of the church's best consideration. Even if the ninety-and-nine were snugly housed in the fold, Smith's soul is still worth the saving.

Should Smith go to Church?

"I don't want to go no furder
Than my Testyment fer that."

Yet Smith does n't care a farthing about the state of his soul. Nothing, in fact, interests him less. Smith's wife had been "brought up in the church," but after her marriage she displayed Smith to the eyes of the congregation for a few Easter Sundays and then gave him up. However, their children attend Sunday school of a denomination other than that in which the Smiths were reared, and Smith gives money to several churches; he declares that he believes churches are a good thing, and he will do almost anything for a church but attend its services. What he really means to say is that he thinks the church is a good thing for Jones and me, but that, as for himself, he gets on comfortably without it.

And the great danger both to the church and to Smith lies in the fact that he does apparently get on so comfortably without it!

I

My personal experiences of religion and of churches have been rather varied, and while

Should Smith go to Church?

they present nothing unusual, I shall refer to them as my justification for venturing to speak to my text at all. I was baptized in the Episcopal Church in infancy, but in about my tenth year I began to gain some knowledge of other Protestant churches. One of my grandfathers had been in turn Methodist and Presbyterian, and I "joined" the latter church in my youth. Becoming later a communicant of the Episcopal Church, I was at intervals a vestryman and a delegate to councils, and for twenty years attended services with a regularity that strikes me as rather admirable in the retrospect.

As a boy I was taken to many "revivals" under a variety of denominational auspices, and later, as a newspaper reporter, I was frequently assigned to conferences and evangelistic meetings. I made my first "hit" as a reporter by my vivacious accounts of the performances of a "trance" revivalist, who operated in a skating-rink in my town. There was something indescribably "woozy" in those cataleptic manifestations in the bare, ill-lighted hall. I even recall vividly the bump of the mourners' heads as they struck the floor, while the evan-

Should Smith go to Church?

gelist moved among the benches haranguing
the crowd. Somewhat earlier I used to delight
in the calisthenic performances of a "boy
preacher" who ranged my part of the world.
His physical activities were as astonishing as his
volubility. At the high moment of his discourse
he would take a flying leap from the platform to
the covered marble baptismal font. He wore
pumps for greater ease in these flights, and
would run the length of the church with astonishing nimbleness, across the backs of the seats
over the heads of the kneeling congregation. I
often listened with delicious horripilations to
the most startling of this evangelist's pero-
rations, in which he described the coming of
the Pale Rider. It was a shuddersome thing.
The horror of it, and the wailing and crying it evoked, come back to me after thirty
years.

The visit of an evangelist used to be an important event in my town; converts were ob-
jects of awed attention, particularly in the case
of notorious hardened sinners whose repentance
awakened the greatest public interest and sympathy. Now that we have passed the quarter-

Should Smith go to Church?

million mark, revivals cause less stir, for evangelists of the more militant, spectacular type seem to avoid the larger cities. Those who have never observed the effect of a religious revival upon a community not too large or too callous to be shaken by it have no idea of the power exerted by the popular evangelist. It is commonly said that these visits only temporarily arrest the march of sin; that after a brief experience of godly life the converts quickly relapse; but I believe that these strident trumpetings of the ram's horn are not without their salutary effect. The saloons, for a time at least, find fewer customers; the forces of decency are strengthened, and the churches usually gain in membership. Most of us prefer our religion without taint of melodrama, but it is far from my purpose to asperse any method or agency that may win men to better ways of life.

At one time and another I seem to have read a good deal on various aspects of religion. Newman and the Tractarians interested me immensely. I purchased all of Newman's writings, and made a collection of his photographs, several of which gaze at me, a little mournfully and rebukingly, as I write; for presently I took a cold plunge into Matthew Arnold, and Rome ceased to call me. Arnold's writings on religious subjects have been obscured by the growing reputation of his poetry; but it was only yesterday that "Literature and Dogma" and "God and the Bible" enjoyed great vogue. He translated continental criticism into terms that made it accessible to laymen, and encouraged liberal thought. He undoubtedly helped many to a new orientation in matters of faith.

My reading in church history, dogma, and criticism has been about that of the average layman. I have enjoyed following the experiments of the psychical researchers, and have been a diligent student of the proceedings of heresy trials. The Andover case and the Briggs controversy once seemed important, and they doubtless were, but they established nothing of value. The churches are warier of heresy trials than they were; and in this connection I hold that a clergyman who entertains an honest doubt as to the virgin birth or the resurrection may still be a faithful servant of Jesus Christ. To unfrock him merely arouses controversy,

Should Smith go to Church?

and draws attention to questions that can never be absolutely determined by any additional evidence likely to be adduced. The continuance in the ministry of a doubter on such points becomes a question of taste which I admit to be debatable; but where, as has happened once in late years, the culprit was an earnest and sincere doer of Christianity's appointed tasks, his conviction served no purpose beyond arousing a species of cynical enjoyment in the bosom of Smith, and of smug satisfaction in those who righteously flung a well-meaning man to the lions.

Far more serious are the difficulties of those ministers of every shade of faith who find themselves curbed and more or less openly threatened for courageously attacking evils they find at their own doors by those responsible for the conditions they assail. Only recently two or three cases have come to my attention of clergymen who had awakened hostility in their congregations by their zeal in social service. The loyal support of such men by their fellows seems to me far nobler than the pursuit of heretics. The Smiths of our country have learned to admire courage in their politics, and there is no reason for believing that they will not rally to a religion that practices it undauntedly. Christ, of all things, was no coward.

There is, I believe, nowhere manifest at this time, within the larger Protestant bodies at least, any disposition to defend the inerrancy of the Bible, and this is fortunate in that it leaves the churches free to deal with more vital matters. It seems fair to assume that criticism has spent its force, and done its worst. The spirit of the Bible has not been harmed by it. The reliance of the Hebrews on the beneficence of Jehovah, the testimony of Jesus to the enduring worth of charity, mercy, and love, have in nowise been injured by textual criticism. The Old Testament, fancifully imagined as the Word of God given by dictation to specially chosen amanuenses, appeals to me no more strongly than a Bible recognized as the vision of brooding spirits, who, in a time when the world was young, and earth was nearer heaven than now, were conscious of longings and dreams that were wonderfully realized in their own hearts and lives. And the essentials of

Should Smith go to Church?

Christ's teachings have lost nothing by criticism.

The Smiths who have drifted away from the churches will hardly be brought back to the pews by even the most scholarly discussion of doubtful texts. Smith is not interested in the authenticity of lines or chapters, nor do nice points of dogma touch the affairs of his life or the needs of his soul. The fact that certain gentlemen in session at Nicæa in A. D. 325 issued a statement of faith for his guidance strikes him as negligible; it does not square with any need of which he is conscious in his own breast.

A church that would regain the lost Smiths will do well to satisfy that large company of the estranged and the indifferent that one need not believe all that is contained between the lids of the Bible to be a Christian. Much of the Bible is vulnerable, but Jesus explained himself in terms whose clarity has in nowise been clouded by criticism. Smith has no time, even if he had the scholarship, to pass upon the merits of the Book of Daniel; but give him Christ's own words without elucidation and he is at once on secure ground. There only lately came into my

Should Smith go to Church?

hands a New Testament in which every utterance of Jesus is given the emphasis of black-face type, with the effect of throwing his sayings into high relief; and no one reading his precepts thus presented can fail to be impressed by the exactness with which He formulated his "secret" into a working platform for the guidance of men. Verily there could be no greater testimony to the divine authority of the Carpenter of Nazareth than the persistence with which his ideal flowers upon the ever-mounting mass of literature produced to explain Him.

II

Smith will not be won back to the church through appeals to theology, or stubborn reaffirmations of creeds and dogmas. I believe it may safely be said that the great body of ministers individually recognize this. A few cling to a superstition that there is inherent in religion itself a power which by some sort of magic, independently of man, will make the faith of Christ triumphant in the world. I do not believe so; Smith could not be made to think so. And Smith's trouble is, if I understand him, not

Should Smith go to Church?

with faith after all, but with works. The church does not impress him as being an efficient machine that yields adequate returns upon the investment. If Smith can be brought to works through faith, well enough; but he is far more critical of works than of faith. Works are within the range of his experience; he admires achievement: show him a foundation of works and interest him in strengthening that foundation and in building upon it, and his faith will take care of itself.

The word we encounter oftenest in the business world nowadays is "efficiency"; the thing of which Smith must first be convinced is that the church may be made efficient. And on that ground he must be met honestly, for Smith is a practical being, who surveys religion, as everything else, with an eye of calculation. At a time when the ethical spirit in America is more healthy and vigorous than ever before, Smith does not connect the movements of which he is aware in business and politics with religion. Religion seems to him to be a poor starved side issue, not a source and guiding spirit in the phenomena he observes and respects.

Should Smith go to Church?

The economic waste represented in church investment and administration does not impress Smith favorably, nor does it awaken admiration in Jones or in me. Smith knows that two groceries on opposite sides of the street are usually one too many. We used to be told that denominational rivalry aroused zeal, but this cannot longer be more than an absurd pretense. This idea that competition is essential to the successful extension of Christianity continues to bring into being many crippled and dying churches, as Smith well knows. And he has witnessed, too, a deterioration of the church's power through its abandonment of philanthropic work to secular agencies, while churches of the familiar type, locked up tight all the week save for a prayer-meeting and choir-practice, have nothing to do. What strikes Smith is their utter wastefulness and futility.

The lack of harmony in individual churches — and there is a good deal of it — is not reassuring to the outsider. The cynical attitude of a good many non-church-going Smiths is due to the strifes, often contemptibly petty, prevailing within church walls. It seems difficult for

Should Smith go to Church?

Christians to dwell together in peace and concord. In almost every congregation there appears to be a party favorable to the minister
and one antagonistic to him. A minister who
seemed to me to fill more fully the Christian
ideal than any man I have known was harassed
in the most brutal fashion by a congregation incapable of appreciating the fidelity and self-
sacrifice that marked his ministry. I recall
with delight the fighting qualities of another
clergyman who was an exceptionally brilliant
pulpit orator. He was a Methodist who had
fallen to the lot of a church that had not lately
been distinguished for able preaching. This
man filled his church twice every Sunday, and
it was the one sought oftenest by strangers
within the city's gates; yet about half his own
membership hated him cordially. Though I was
never of his flock, I enjoyed his sermons; and
knowing something of his relations with the opposition party in his congregation, I recall with
keenest pleasure how he fought back. Now and
then an arrow grazed his ear; but he was un-
heedful of warnings that he would be pilloried
for heresy. He landed finally in his old age in

132

an obscure church, where he died, still fighting with his back to the wall. Though the shepherd's crook as a weapon is going out of style, I have an idea that clergymen who stand sturdily for their own ideals receive far kindlier consideration than those who meekly bow to vestries, trustees, deacons, elders, and bishops.

Music has long been notoriously a provoker of discord. Once in my news-hunting days I suffered the ignominy of a "scoop" on a choir-rumpus, and I thereupon formed the habit of lending an anxious ear to rumors of trouble in choir-lofts. The average ladder-like *Te Deum*, built up for the display of the soprano's vocal prowess, has always struck me as an unholy thing. I even believe that the horrors of highly embellished offertories have done much to tighten purse-strings and deaden generous impulses. The presence behind the pulpit of a languid quartette praising God on behalf of the bored sinners in the pews has always seemed to me the profanest of anomalies. Nor has long contemplation of vested choirs in Episcopal churches shaken my belief that church music should be an affair of the congregation.

Should Smith go to Church?

There seems to exist inevitably, even in the smallest congregation, "a certain rich man" whose opinions must be respected by the pulpit. The minister of a large congregation confessed to me despairingly, not long ago, that the courage had been taken out of him by the protests evoked whenever he touched even remotely upon social topics like child labor, or shorter hours for workingmen. There were manufacturers in that church who would not "stand for it." Ministers are warned that they must attend to their own business, which is preaching the Word of God not so concretely or practically as to offend the "pillars."

Just what is it, I wonder, that a minister may preach without hazarding his job? It is said persistently that the trouble with the church at the present day is that the ministers no longer preach the Word of God; that if Christian Truth were again taught with the old vigor, people would hear it gladly. This is, I believe, an enormous fallacy. I know churches where strict orthodoxy has been preached uninterruptedly for years, and which have steadily declined in spite of it — or because of it. Not

134

Should Smith go to Church?

long ago, in a great assembly of one of the strongest denominations, when that cry for a return to the "Old Bible Truth" was raised, one minister rose and attacked the plea, declaring that he had never faltered in his devotion to ancient dogma, and yet his church was dying. And even so, many churches whose walls echo uninterruptedly an absolutely impeccable orthodoxy are failing. We shall not easily persuade Smith to forego the golf-links on Sunday morning to hear the "Old Gospel Truth" preached in out-worn, meaningless phrases. Those old coins have the gold in them, but they must be recast in new moulds if they are again to pass current.

III

The difficulties of the clergy are greatly multiplied in these days. The pulpit has lost its old authority. It no longer necessarily follows that the ministers are the men of greatest cultivation in their community. The Monday morning newspapers formerly printed, in my town, pretty full excerpts of sermons. I recall the case of one popular minister whose sermons continued to be printed long after he had removed to another city. Nowadays nothing from the pulpit that is not sensational is considered worth printing. And the parson has lost his social importance, moving back slowly toward his old place below the salt. He used to be "asked," even if he was not sincerely "expected" at the functions given by his parishioners; but this has changed now that fewer families have any parson to invite.

A minister's is indubitably the hardest imaginable lot. Every one criticizes him. He is abused for illiberality, or, seeking to be all things to all men, he is abused for consorting with sinners. His door-bell tinkles hourly, and he must answer the behest of people he does not know, to marry or bury people he never heard of. He is expected to preach eloquently, to augment his flock, to keep a hand on the Sunday school, to sit on platforms in the interest of all good causes, and to bear himself with discretion amid the tortuous mazes of church and secular politics. There seem to be, in churches of all kinds, ambitious pontiffs — lay popes — possessed of an ambition to hold both their fel-

Should Smith go to Church?

low laymen and their meek, long-suffering minister in subjection. Why anyone should wish to be a church boss I do not know; and yet the supremacy is sometimes won after a struggle that has afforded the keenest delight to the cynical Smiths on the outside. One must view these internecine wars more in sorrow than in anger. They certainly contribute not a little to popular distrust of the church as a conservator of love and peace.

There are men in the ministry who can have had no clear vocation to the clerical life; but there are misfits and failures in all professions. Some of these, through bigotry or stupidity, do much to justify Smith's favorite dictum that there is as much Christianity outside the church as within it. Now and then I find a Smith whose distrust of religion is based upon some disagreeable adventure with a clergyman, and I can't deny that my own experiences with the cloth have been, on one or two occasions, disturbing. As to the more serious of these I may not speak, but I shall mention two incidents, for the reason that they are such trifles as affect Smith with joy. Once in a parish-meeting I saw

Should Smith go to Church?

a bishop grossly humiliated for having undertaken to rebuke a young minister for wearing a chasuble, or not wearing it, or for removing it in the pulpit, or the other way round,—at any rate, it was some such momentous point in ecclesiastical millinery that had loosened a frightful fury of recrimination. The very sight or suggestion of chasubles has ever since awakened in me the most unchristian resentment. While we fought over the chasuble I suppose people actually died within bow-shot of the church without knowing that "if any man sin we have an advocate with the Father, Jesus Christ the Righteous."

And speaking of bishops, I venture the interpolation that that office, believed by many to be the softest berth in Zion as it exists in the Episcopal Church, is in fact the most vexatious and thankless to which any man can aspire; nor have I in mind the laborious lives of adventurous spirits like Whipple, Hare, and Rowe, but others who carry the burdens of established dioceses, where the troubles of one minister are multiplied upon the apostolic head by the number of parishes in his jurisdiction.

Should Smith go to Church?

Again, at a summer resort on our North Atlantic Coast once familiar to me, there stood, within reach of fierce seas, one of the most charming of churches. It was sought daily by visitors, and many women, walking the shore, used to pause there to rest, for prayer, or out of sheer curiosity. And yet it appeared that no woman might venture into this edifice hatless. The *locum tenens*, recalling St. Paul's question whether it is "comely that a woman pray unto God uncovered," was so outraged by the visits of hatless women to the church that he tacked a notice on the door setting forth in severe terms that, whereas men should enter the church bareheaded, women should not desecrate the temple by entering uncovered. I remember that when I had read that warning, duly signed with the clergyman's name, I sat down on the rocks and looked at the ocean for a long time, marveling that a sworn servant of God, consecrated in his service by the apostles' successors, able to spend a couple of months at one of the pleasantest summer resorts in America, should have been horror-struck at the unholy intrusion of a hatless girl in his church, when people in

139

the hot city he had fled suffered and died, ignorant of the very name of Christ.

IV

"My church home" is an old phrase one still hears in communities whose social life is not yet wholly divorced from the church. There is something pleasant and reassuring in the sound of it; and I do not believe we shall ever have in America an adequate substitute for that tranquility and peace which are still observable in towns where the church retains its hold upon the larger part of the community, and where it exercises a degree of compulsion upon men and women who find in its life a faith and hope that have proved not the least strong of the bulwarks of democracy. In wholly strange towns I have experienced the sense of this in a way I am reluctant to think wholly sentimental. Where, on crisp winter evenings, the young people come trooping happily in from the meetings of their own auxiliary societies, where vim and energy are apparent in the gathering congregation, and where one sees with half an eye that the pastor is a true leader and shepherd of his

140

flock — in such a picture there must be, for many of us, something that lays deep hold upon the heart. They are not concerned in such gatherings with higher criticism, but with cleanness and wholesomeness of life, and with that faith, never to be too closely scrutinized or analyzed, that "singeth low in every heart."

One might weep to think how rare those pictures must become — one might weep if there were not the great problems now forced upon us, of chance and change, that drive home to all thinking men and women the great need of infusing the life of the spirit into our industrial and political struggles. If, in the end, our great experiment in self-government fail, it will be through the loss of those spiritual forces which from the beginning have guided and ruled us. It is only lately that we have begun to hear of Christian socialism, and a plausible phrase it is; but true democracy seems to me essentially Christian. When we shall have thoroughly christianized our democracy, and democratized our Christianity, we shall not longer yield to moods of despair, or hearken to prophets of woe.

Should Smith go to Church?

The Smith for whom I presume to speak is not indifferent to the call of revitalized democracy. He has confessed to me his belief that the world is a kindlier place, and that more agencies of helpfulness are at work, than ever before; and to restore the recalcitrant Smith to the church it is necessary first of all to convince him that the church honestly seeks to be the chief of such agencies. The Young Men's Christian Association, the Charity Organization Society, and the Settlement House all afford outlets for Smith's generous benevolences. And it was a dark day for the church when she allowed these multiplying philanthropies to slip away from her. Smith points to them with a flourish, and says that he prefers to give his money where it is put to practical use. To him the church is an economic parasite, doing business on one day of the week, immune from taxation, and the last of his neighbors to scrape the snow from her sidewalks! The fact that there are within fifteen minutes' walk of his house half a dozen churches, all struggling to maintain themselves, and making no appreciable impression upon the community, is not

Should Smith go to Church?

lost upon Smith, — the practical, unemotional, busy Smith. Smith speaks to me with sincere admiration of his friend, the Salvation Army major, to whom he opens his purse ungrudgingly; but the church over the way — that grim expensive pile of stone, closed for all but five or six hours of the week! — Smith shakes his head ruefully when you suggest it. It is to him a bad investment that ought to be turned over to a receiver for liquidation.

Smith's wife has derived bodily and spiritual help from Christian Science, and Smith speaks with respect of that cult. He is half persuaded that there must be something in it. A great many of the Smiths who never had a church tie, or who gave up church-going, have allied themselves with Christian Science, — what many of Mrs. Eddy's followers in familiar talk abbreviate as "Science," as though Science were the more important half of it. This proves at least that the Smiths are not averse to some sort of spiritual food, or quite clearly demonstrates a dissatisfaction with the food they had formerly received. It proves also that the old childlike faith in miracles is still possible even in our

Should Smith go to Church?

generation. Christian Science struts in robes of prosperity in my bailiwick, and its followers pain and annoy me only by their cheerful assumption that they have just discovered God.

Smith's plight becomes, then, more serious the more we ponder his case; but the plight of the church is not less grave to those who, feeling that Christianity has still its greatest work to do, are anxious for its rejuvenation. As to whether the church should go to Smith, or Smith should seek the church, there can be no debate. Smith will not seek the church; it must be on the church's initiative that he is restored to it. The Layman's Forward Movement testifies to the awakened interest of the churches in Smith. As I pen these pages I pick up a New York newspaper and find on the pages devoted to sports an advertisement signed by the Men and Religion Forward Movement, calling attention to the eight hundred and eighty churches, Protestant and Catholic, and the one hundred and seven synagogues in the metropolis, — the beginning, I believe, of a campaign of advertising on sporting pages. I repeat, that I wish to belittle no honest effort in any quarter or under

144

any auspices to interest men in the spiritual life; but I cannot forbear mentioning that Smith has already smiled disagreeably at this effort to catch his attention. Still, if Smith, looking for the baseball score, is reminded that the church is interested in his welfare, I am not one to sit in the scorner's seat.

V

A panacea for the ills of the church is something no one expects to find; and those who are satisfied with the church as it stands, and believe it to be unmenaced by danger, — who see the Will of God manifested even in Smith's disaffection, will not be interested in my opinion that, of all the suggestions that have been made for the renewal of the church's life, church union, upon the broadest lines, directed to the increase of the church's efficiency in spiritual and social service, is the one most likely to bring Smith back to the fold. Moreover, I believe that Smith's aid should be invoked in the business of unification, for the reason that on patriotic grounds, if no other, he is vitally concerned in the welding of Christianity and democracy more firmly together. Church union has long been the despair and the hope of many sincere, able, and devoted men, who have at heart the best interests of Christendom, and it is impossible that any great number of Protestants except the most bigoted reactionaries can distrust the results of union.

The present crisis — for it is not less than that — calls for more immediate action by all concerned than seems imminent. We have heard for many years that "in God's own time" union would be effected; and yet union is far from being realized. The difficulty of operating through councils and conventions is manifest. These bodies move necessarily and properly with great deliberation. Before the great branches of Protestantism have reconciled their differences, and agreed upon a *modus vivendi*, it is quite possible that another ten or twenty years may pass; and in the present state of the churches, time is of the essence of preservation and security.

While we await action by the proposed World Conference for the consideration of questions touching "faith and order," much can be done toward crystallizing sentiment favorable to union. A letter has been issued to its clergy by the Episcopal Church, urging such profitable use of the interval of waiting; and I dare say the same spirit prevails in other communions. A purely sentimental union will not suffice, nor is the question primarily one for theologians or denominational partisans, but for those who believe that there is inherent in the method and secret of Jesus something very precious that is now seriously jeopardized, and that the time is at hand for saving it, and broadening and deepening the channel through which it reaches mankind.

VI

In the end, unity, if it ever take practical form, must become a local question. This is certainly true in so far as the urban field is concerned, and I may say in parenthesis that, in my own state, the country churches are already practicing a kind of unification, in regions where the automobile and the interurban railway make it possible for farm and village folk to run into town to church. Many rural churches have been abandoned and boarded up, their congregations in this way forming new religious and social units. I suggest that in towns and cities where the weaknesses resulting from denominational rivalry are most apparent, the problems of unification be taken up in a purely local way. I propose the appointment of local commissions, representative of all Protestant bodies, to study the question and devise plans for increasing the efficiency of existing churches, and to consider ways and means of bringing the church into vital touch with the particular community under scrutiny. This should be done in a spirit of absolute honesty, without envy, hatred, or malice. The test of service should be applied relentlessly, and every religious society should make an honest showing of its conditions and needs.

Upon the trial-balance thus struck there should be, wherever needed, an entirely new redistribution of church property, based wholly upon local and neighborhood needs. For example, the familiar, badly housed, struggling mission in an industrial centre would be able at once to anticipate the fruits of years of labor, through the elimination of unnecessary

Should Smith go to Church?

churches in quarters already over-supplied. Not only should body and soul be cared for in the vigorous institutional church, the church of the future, but there is no reason why the programme should not include theatrical entertainments, concerts, and dances. Many signs encourage the belief that the drama has a great future in America, and the reorganized, redistributed churches might well seize upon it as a powerful auxiliary and ally. Scores of motion-picture shows in every city testify to the growing demand for amusement, and they conceal much mischief; and the public dance-house is a notorious breeder of vice.

Let us consider that millions of dollars are invested in American churches, which are, in the main, open only once or twice a week, and that fear of defiling the temple is hardly justification for the small amount of actual service performed by the greater number of churches of the old type. By introducing amusements, the institutional church — the "department church," if you like — would not only meet a need, but it would thus eliminate many elements of competition. The people living about a strong institutional church would find it, in a new sense, "a church home." The doors should stand open seven days in the week to "all such as have erred and are deceived"; and men and women should be waiting at the portals "to comfort and help the weak-hearted; and to raise up those who fall."

If in a dozen American cities having from fifty thousand to two or three hundred thousand inhabitants, this practical local approach toward union should be begun in the way indicated, the data adduced would at least be of importance to the convocations that must ultimately pass upon the question. Just such facts and figures as could be collected by local commissions would naturally be required, finally, in any event; and much time would be saved by anticipating the call for such reports.

I am familiar with the argument that many sorts of social service are better performed by non-sectarian societies, and we have all witnessed the splendid increase of secular effort in lines feebly attacked and relinquished, as though with a grateful sigh, by the churches. When the Salvation Army's trumpet and drum

Should Smith go to Church?

first sounded in the market-place, we were told that that valiant organization could do a work impossible for the churches; when the Settlement House began to appear in American cities, that, too, was undertaking something better left to the sociologist. Those prosperous organizations of Christian young men and women, whose investment in property in our American cities is now very great, are, also, we are assured, performing a service which the church could not properly have undertaken. Charity long ago moved out of the churches, and established headquarters in an office with typewriter and telephone.

If it is true that the service here indicated is better performed by secular organizations, why is it that the power of the church has steadily waned ever since these losses began? Certainly there is little in the present state of American Protestantism to afford comfort to those who believe that a one-day-a-week church, whose apparatus is limited to a pulpit in the auditorium, and a map of the Holy Land in the Sunday-school room, is presenting a veritable, living Christ to the hearts and imaginations of men.

Should Smith go to Church?

And on the bright side of the picture it should be said that nothing in the whole field of Christian endeavor is more encouraging or inspiring than an examination of the immense social service performed under the auspices of various religious organizations in New York City. This has been particularly marked in the Episcopal Church. The late Bishop Potter, and his successor in the metropolitan diocese, early gave great impetus to social work, and those who contend that the church's sole business is to preach the Word of God will find a new revelation of the significance of that Word by a study of the labors of half a dozen parishes that exemplify every hour of every day the possibilities of efficient Christian democracy.

The church has lost ground that perhaps never can be recovered. Those who have established secular settlements for the poor, or those who have created homes for homeless young men and women, can hardly be asked to "pool" and divide their property with the churches. But, verily, even with all the many agencies now at work to ameliorate distress and uplift the fallen, the fields continue white already to the harvest, and the laborers are few. With the church revitalized, and imbued with the spirit of utility and efficiency so potent in our time, it may plant its wavering banner securely on new heights. It may show that all these organizations that have sapped its strength, and diminished the force of its testimony before men, have derived their inspiration from Him who came out of Nazareth to lighten all the world.

VII

The reorganization of the churches along the line I have indicated would work hardship on many ministers. It would not only mean that many clergymen would find themselves seriously disturbed in positions long held under the old order, but that preparation for the ministry would necessarily be conducted along new lines. The training that now fits a student to be the pastor of a one-day-a-week church would be worthless in a unified and socialized church.

"There are diversities of gifts"; but "it is the same God which worketh all in all." In the departmental church, with its chapel or temple fitly adorned, the preaching of Christ's message

153

Should Smith go to Church?

would not be done by a weary minister worn by the thousand vexatious demands upon a minister's time, but by one specially endowed with the preaching gift. In this way the prosperous congregation would not enjoy a monopoly of good preaching. Men gifted in pastoral work would specialize in that, and the relationship between the church and the home, which has lost its old fineness and sweetness, would be restored. Men trained in that field would direct the undertakings frankly devised to provide recreation and amusement. Already the schoolhouse in our cities is being put to social use; in the branch libraries given by Mr. Carnegie to my city, assembly-rooms and kitchens are provided to encourage social gatherings; and here is another opportunity still open to the church if it hearken to the call of the hour.

In this unified and rehabilitated church of which I speak, — the every-day-in-the-week church, open to all sorts and conditions of men, — what would become of the creeds and the old theology? I answer this first of all by saying that coalition in itself would be a supreme demonstration of the enduring power and glory of

Should Smith go to Church?

Christianity. Those who are jealous for the integrity of the ancient faith would manifestly have less to defend, for the church would be speaking for herself in terms understood of all men. The seven-day church, being built upon efficiency and aiming at definite results, could afford to suffer men to think as they liked on the virgin birth, the miracles, and the resurrection of the body, if they faithfully practiced the precepts of Jesus.

This busy, helpful, institutional church, welcoming under one roof men of all degrees, to broaden, sweeten, and enlighten their lives, need ask no more of those who accept its service than that they believe in a God who ever lives and loves, and in Christ, who appeared on earth in His name to preach justice, mercy, charity, and kindness. I should not debate metaphysics through a barred wicket with men who needed the spiritual or physical help of the church, any more than my neighbor, Smith, that prince of good fellows, would ask a hungry tramp to saw a cord of wood before he gave him his breakfast.

Questions of liturgy can hardly be a bar, nor can the validity of Christian orders in one body or another weigh heavily with any who are sincerely concerned for the life of the church and the widening of its influence. "And other sheep I have, which are not of this fold: them also I must bring, and they shall hear my voice; and they shall become one flock, one shepherd." I have watched ministers in practically every Christian church take bread and break it, and bless the cup, and offer it in the name of Jesus, and I have never been able to feel that the sacrament was not as efficacious when received reverently from one as from another.

If wisdom and goodness are God, then foolish, indeed, is he who would "misdefine these till God knows them no more." The unified seven-day church would neglect none of "the weightier matters of the law, justice and mercy and faith," in the collecting of tithe of mint and anise and cummin. It would not deny its benefits to those of us who are unblest with deep spiritual perception, for it is by the grace of God that we are what we are. "I will pray with the spirit, and I will pray with the understanding also: I will sing with the spirit and I will sing with the understanding also. Else if thou bless with the spirit, how shall he that filleth the place of the unlearned say the Amen at thy giving of thanks, seeing he knoweth not what thou sayest?"

"Hath man no second life? — *Pitch this one high!*
    Sits there no judge in Heaven our sins to see? —
More strictly, then, the inward judge obey!
Was Christ a man like us? *Ah, let us try*
    If we, then, too, can be such men as he!"

Somewhere there is a poem that relates the experience of a certain humble priest, who climbed the steeple of his church to commune more nearly with God. And, as he prayed, he heard the Voice answering, and asked, "Where art thou, Lord?" and the Lord replied, "Down here, among my people!"

The Tired Business Man

The Tired Business Man

I

SMITH flashed upon me unexpectedly in
Berlin. It was nearly a year ago, just before the summer invasion of tourists, and I was
reading the letters of a belated mail over my
coffee, when I was aroused by an unmistakable
American voice demanding water. I turned
and beheld, in a sunny alcove at the end of the
restaurant, my old friend Smith who had
dropped his newspaper for the purpose of ar-
raigning a frightened and obtuse waiter for his
inability to grasp the idea that persons in ordi-
nary health, and reasonably sane, do, at times,
use water as a beverage. It was not merely the
alarmed waiter and all his tribe that Smith
execrated: he swept Prussia and the German
Empire into the limbo of lost nations. Mrs.
Smith begged him to be calm, offering the plausible suggestion that the waiter could n't understand a word of English. She appealed to a
third member of the breakfast party, a young

161

The Tired Business Man

lady, whose identity had puzzled me for a moment. It seemed incredible that this could be the Smiths' Fanny, whom I had dandled on my knee in old times, — and yet a second glance convinced me that the young person was no unlikely realization of the promise of the Fanny who had ranged our old neighborhood at "home" and appalled us, even at five, by her direct and pointed utterances. If the child may be mother to the woman, this was that identical Fanny. I should have known it from the cool fashion in which she dominated the situation, addressing the relieved waiter in his own tongue, with the result that he fled precipitately in search of water — and ice, if any, indeed, were obtainable — for the refreshment of these eccentric Americans.

When I crossed to their table I found Smith still growling while he tried to find his lost place in the New York stock market in his London newspaper. My appearance was the occasion for a full recital of his wrongs, in that amusing hyperbole which is so refreshing in all the Smiths I know. He begged me to survey the table, that I might enjoy his triumph in having

The Tired Business Man

been able to surmount local prejudice and pro-
cure for himself what he called a breakfast of
civilized food. The continental breakfast was
to him an odious thing: he announced his intention of exposing it; he meant to publish its
iniquity to the world and drive it out of business. Mrs. Smith laughed nervously. She appeared anxious and distraught and I was smit-
ten with pity for her. But there was a twinkle
in Miss Smith's eye, a smile about her pretty
lips, that discounted heavily the paternal fury.
She communicated, with a glance, a sense of her
own attitude toward her father's indignation:
it did not matter a particle; it was merely
funny, that was all, that her father, who demanded and commanded all things on his own
soil, should here be helpless to obtain a drop of
cold water with which to slake his thirst when
every one knew that he could have bought the
hotel itself with a scratch of the pen. When
Smith asked me to account for the prevalence of
hydrophobia in Europe it was really for the joy
of hearing his daughter laugh. And it is well
worth anyone's while to evoke laughter from
Fanny. For Fanny is one of the prettiest girls

The Tired Business Man

in the world, one of the cleverest, one of the most interesting and amusing.

As we lingered at the table (water with ice having arrived and the Stars and Stripes flying triumphantly over the pitcher), I was brought up to date as to the recent history of the Smiths. As an old neighbor from home they welcomed me to their confidence. The wife and daughter had been abroad a year with Munich as their chief base. Smith's advent had been unexpected and disturbing. Rest and change having been prescribed, he had jumped upon a steamer and the day before our encounter had joined his wife and daughter in Berlin. They were waiting now for a conference with a German neurologist to whom Smith had been consigned — in desperation, I fancied — by his American doctor. Mrs. Smith's distress was as evident as his own irritation; Miss Fanny alone seemed wholly tranquil. She ignored the apparent gravity of the situation and assured me that her father had at last decided upon a long vacation. She declared that if her father per-

The Tired Business Man

sisted in his intention of sailing for New York
three weeks later, she and her mother would
accompany him.

While we talked a cablegram was brought to
Smith; he read it and frowned. Mrs. Smith met
my eyes and shook her head; Fanny frugally
subtracted two thirds of the silver Smith was
leaving on the tray as a tip and slipped it into
her purse. It was a handsome trinket, the
purse; Fanny's appointments all testified to
Smith's prosperity and generosity. I remembered these friends so well in old times, when
they lived next door to me in the Mid-Western
town which Smith, ten years before, had out-
grown and abandoned. His income had in my
observation jumped from two to twenty thousand, and no one knew now to what fabulous
height it had climbed. He was one of the men
to reckon with in the larger affairs of "Big
Business." And here was the wife who had
shared his early struggles, and the child born of
those contented years, and here was Smith,
with whom in the old days I had smoked my
after-breakfast cigar on the rear platform of a
street car in our town, that we then thought the

The Tired Business Man

"best town on earth," — here were my old neighbors in a plight that might well tax the renowned neurologist's best powers.

What had happened to Smith? I asked myself; and the question was also in his wife's wondering eyes. And as we dallied, Smith fingered his newspaper fretfully while I answered his wife's questions about our common acquaintances at "home" as she still called our provincial capital.

It was not my own perspicacity but Fanny's which subsequently made possible an absolute diagnosis of Smith's case, somewhat before the cautious German specialist had announced it. From data supplied by Fanny I arrived at the conclusion that Smith is the "tired business man," and only one of a great number of American Smiths afflicted with the same malady, — bruised, nerve-worn victims of our malignant gods of success. The phrase, as I shall employ it here, connotes not merely the type of iron-gray stock broker with whom we have been made familiar by our American drama of business and politics, but his brother (also prematurely gray and a trifle puffy under the eyes)

The Tired Business Man

found sedulously burning incense before Mammon in every town of one hundred thousand souls in America. I am not sure, on reflection, that he is not visible in thriving towns of twenty-five thousand, — or wherever "collateral" and "discount" are established in the local idiom and the cocktail is a medium of commercial and social exchange. The phenomena presented by my particular Smith are similar to those observed in those lesser Smiths who are the restless and dissatisfied biggest frogs in smaller puddles. Even the farmers are tired of contemplating their glowing harvests and bursting barns and are moving to town to rest.

III

Is it possible that tired men really wield a considerable power and influence in these American States so lately wrested from savagery? Confirmation of this reaches us through many channels. In politics we are assured that the tired business man is a serious obstructionist in the path of his less prosperous and less weary brethren engaged upon the pursuit of happiness and capable of enjoying it in successes that would seem contemptibly meagre to Smith. Thousands of Smiths who have not yet ripened for the German specialists are nevertheless tired enough to add to the difficulty of securing so simple a thing as reputable municipal government. It is because of Smith's weariness and apathy that we are obliged to confess that no decent man will accept the office of mayor in our American cities.

In my early acquaintance with Smith — in those simple days when he had time to loaf in my office and talk politics — an ardent patriotism burned in him. He was proud of his ancestors who had not withheld their hand all the way from Lexington to Yorktown, and he used to speak with emotion of that dark winter at Valley Forge. He would look out of the window upon Washington Street and declare, with a fine sweep of the hand, that "We've got to keep all this; we've got to keep it for these people and for our children." He had not been above sitting as delegate in city and state conventions, and he had once narrowly escaped a nomination for the legislature. The industry he owned and managed was a small affair and he knew all the

The Tired Business Man

employees by name. His lucky purchase of a patent that had been kicked all over the United States before the desperate inventor offered it to him had sent his fortunes spinning into millions within ten years. Our cautious banker who had vouchsafed Smith a reasonable guarded credit in the old days had watched, with the mild cynical smile peculiar to conservative bank presidents, the rapid enrollment of Smith's name in the lists of directors of some of the solidest corporations known to Wall Street. It is a long way from Washington Street to Wall Street, and men who began life with more capital than Smith never cease marveling at the ease with which he effected the transition. Some who continue where he left them in the hot furrows stare gloomily after him and exclaim upon the good luck that some men have. Smith's abrupt taking-off would cause at least a momentary chill in a thousand safety-vault boxes. Smith's patriotism, which in the old days, when he liked to speak of America as the republic of the poor, and when he knew most of the "Commemoration Ode" and all of the "Gettysburg Address" by heart, is far more

The Tired Business Man

concrete than it used to be. When Smith visits
Washington during the sessions of Congress the
country is informed of it. It is he who scrutin-
izes new senators and passes upon their trust-
worthiness. And it was Smith who, after one of
these inspections, said of a member of our upper
chamber that, "He's all right; he speaks our
language," meaning not the language of the
"Commemoration Ode" or the "Gettysburg
Address," but a recondite dialect understood
only at the inner gate of the money-changers.

IV

No place was ever pleasanter in the old days
than the sitting-room of Smith's house. It was
the coziest of rooms and gave the lie to those
who have maintained that civilization is impossible around a register. A happy, contented
family life existed around that square of per-
forated iron in the floor of the Smiths' sitting-
room. In the midst of arguments on life, letters,
the arts, politics, and what-not, Smith would,
as the air grew chill toward midnight, and
when Mrs. Smith went to forage for refresh-
ments in the pantry, descend to the cellar to

The Tired Business Man

renew the flagging fires of the furnace with his own hands. The purchase of a new engraving, the capture of a rare print, was an event to be celebrated by the neighbors. We went to the theatre sometimes, and kept track of the affairs of the stage; and lectures and concerts were not beneath us. Mrs. Smith played Chopin charmingly on a piano Smith had given her for a Christmas present when Fanny was three. They were not above belonging to our neighborhood book and magazine club, and when they bought a book it was a good one. I remember our discussions of George Meredith and Hardy and Howells, and how we saved Stockton's stories to enjoy reading them in company around the register. A trip to New York was an event for the Smiths in those days as well as for the rest of us, to be delayed until just the right moment for seeing the best plays, and an opera, with an afternoon carefully set apart for the Metropolitan Museum. We were glad the Smiths could go, even if the rest of us could n't; for they told us all so generously of their adventures when they came back! They kept a "horse and buggy," and

The Tired Business Man

Mrs. Smith used to drive to the factory with Fanny perched beside her to bring Smith home at the end of his day's work.

In those days the Smiths presented a picture before which one might be pardoned for lingering in admiration. I shall resent any suggestions that I am unconsciously writing them down as American *bourgeois* with the contemptuous insinuations that are conveyed by that term. Nor were they Philistines, but sound, wholesome, cheerful Americans, who bought their eggs direct from "the butterman" and kept a jug of buttermilk in the icebox. I assert that Smiths of their type were and are, wherever they still exist, an encouragement and a hope to all who love their America. They are the Americans to whom Lincoln became as one of Plutarch's men, and for whom Longfellow wrote "The Children's Hour," and on whom Howells smiles quizzically and with complete understanding. Thousands of us knew thousands of these Smiths only a few years ago, all the way from Portland, Maine, to Portland, Oregon. I linger upon them affectionately as I have known and loved them in

172

The Tired Business Man

the Ohio Valley, but I have enjoyed glimpses of them in Kansas City and Omaha, Minneapolis and Detroit, and know perfectly well that I should find them realizing to the full life, liberty, and the pursuit of happiness in many other regions, — for example, with only slight differences of background, in Richmond, Virginia, and Burlington, Vermont. And in all these places some particular Smith is always moving to Chicago or Boston or New York on his way to a sanatorium or Bad Neuheim and a German specialist! Innumerable Smiths, not yet so prosperous as the old friend I encountered in Berlin, are abandoning their flower-gardens and the cozy verandas (sacred to neighborhood confidences on the long summer evenings) and their gusty registers for compact and steam-heated apartments with only the roof-garden overhead as a breathing-place.

There seems to be no field in which the weary Smith is not exercising a baneful influence. We have fallen into the habit of laying many of our national sins at his door, and usually with reason. His hand is hardly concealed as he thrusts it nervously through the curtains of legislative

The Tired Business Man

chambers, state and national. He invades city halls and corrupts municipal councils. Even the fine arts are degraded for his pleasure. Smith, it seems, is too weary from his day's work to care for dramas

"That bear a weighty and a serious brow,
Sad, high, and working, full of state and woe."

He is one of the loyalest patrons of that type of beguilement known as the "musical comedy," which in its most engaging form is a naughty situation sprinkled with cologne water and set to waltz time. Still, if he dines at the proper hour at a Fifth Avenue restaurant and eats more and drinks more than he should (to further the hardening of his arteries for the German specialist), he may arrive late and still hear the tune everyone on Broadway is whistling. The girl behind the book-counter knows Smith a mile off, and hands him at once a novel that has a lot of "go" to it, or one wherein "smart" people assembled in house-parties for week-ends, amuse themselves by pinning pink ribbons on the Seventh Commandment. If the illustrations are tinted and the first page opens

The Tired Business Man

upon machine-gun dialogue, the sale is effected
all the more readily. Or, reluctant to tackle a
book of any sort, he may gather up a few of
those magazines whose fiction jubilantly em-
phasizes the least noble passions of man. And
yet my Smith delighted, in those old days
around the register, in Howells's clean, firm
stroke; and we were always quoting dear Stockton — "black stockings for sharks" — "put
your board money in the ginger jar." What
a lot of silly, happy, comfortable geese we
were!

It seems only yesterday that the first trayful
of cocktails jingled into a parlor in my town as
a prelude to dinner; and I recall the scandalous
reports of that innovation which passed up and
down the maple-arched thoroughfares that give
so sober and cloistral an air to our residential
area. When that first tray appeared at our
elbows, just before that difficult moment when
we gentlemen of the provinces, rather conscious at all times of our dress-coats, are wondering whether it is the right or left arm we
should offer the lady we are about to take in,
we were startled, as though the Devil had in-

vaded the domestic sanctuary and perched
himself on the upright piano. Nothing is more
depressing than the thought that all these
Smiths, many of whose fathers slept in the
rain and munched hard-tack for a principle in
the sixties, are unable to muster an honest
appetite, but must pucker their stomachs with
a tonic before they can swallow their daily
bread. Perhaps our era's great historian will
be a stomach specialist whose pages, bristling
with statistics and the philosophy thereof, will
illustrate the undermining and honeycombing
of our institutions by gin and bitters.

v

The most appalling thing about us Americans
is our complete sophistication. The English are
children. An Englishman is at no moment so
delightful as when he lifts his brows and says
"Really!" The Frenchman at his sidewalk
table watches the world go by with unwearied
delight. At any moment Napoleon may appear;
or he may hear great news of a new drama, or
the latest lion of the salon may stroll by. Awe
and wonder are still possible in the German,

The Tired Business Man

bred as he is upon sentiment and fairy-lore: the Italian is beautifully credulous. On my first visit to Paris, having arrived at midnight and been established in a hotel room that hung above a courtyard which I felt confident had witnessed the quick thrusts of Porthos, Athos, and Aramis, I wakened at an early hour to the voice of a child singing in the area below. It has always seemed to me that that artless song flung out upon the bright charmed morning came from the very heart of France! France, after hundreds of years of achievement, prodigious labor, and staggering defeat, is still a child among the nations.

Only the other day I attended a prize-fight in Paris. It was a gay affair held in a huge amphitheatre and before a great throng of spectators of whom a third were women. The match was for twenty rounds between a Frenchman and an Australian negro. After ten rounds it was pretty clear that the negro was the better man; and my lay opinion was supported by the judgment of two American journalists, sounder critics than I profess to be of the merits of such contests. The decision was, of course, in favor

The Tired Business Man

of the Frenchman and the cheering was vociferous and prolonged. And it struck me as a fine thing that that crowd could cheer so lustily the wrong decision! It was that same spirit that led France forth jauntily against Bismarck's bayonets. I respect the emotion with which a Frenchman assures me that one day French soldiers will plant the tri-color on the Brandenburg Gate. He dreams of it as a child dreams of to-morrow's games.

But we are at once the youngest and the oldest of the nations. We are drawn to none but the "biggest" shows, and hardly cease yawning long enough to be thrilled by the consummating leap of death across the four rings where folly has already disproved all natural laws. The old prayer, "Make me a child again just for to-night," has vanished with the belief in Santa Claus. No American really wants to be a child again. It was with a distinct shock that I heard recently a child of five telephoning for an automobile in a town that had been threatened by hostile Indians not more than thirty years ago. Our children avail themselves with the coolest condescension of all the apparatus of our com-

178

The Tired Business Man

plex modern life: they are a thousand years old the day they are born.

The farmer who once welcomed the lightning-rod salesman as a friend of mankind is moving to town now and languidly supervising the tilling of his acres from an automobile. One of these vicarious husbandmen, established in an Indiana county seat, found it difficult to employ his newly acquired leisure. The automobile had not proved itself a toy of unalloyed delight, and the feet that had followed unwearied the hay rake and plow faltered upon the treads of the mechanical piano. He began to alternate motor flights with more deliberate drives behind a handsome team of blacks. The eyes of the town undertaker fell in mortal envy upon that team and he sought to buy it. The tired husbandman felt that here, indeed, was an opportunity to find light gentlemanly occupation, while at the same time enjoying the felicities of urban life, so he consented to the use of his horses, but with the distinct understanding that he should be permitted to drive the hearse!

The Tired Business Man

VI

If we are not, after all, a happy people, in the full enjoyment of life and liberty, what is this sickness that troubleth our Israel? Why huddle so many captains within the walls of the city, impotently whining beside their spears? Why seek so many for rest while this our Israel is young among the nations? " Thou hast multiplied the nation and not increased the joy; they joy before thee according to the joy in harvest and as men rejoice when they divide the spoil." Weariness fell upon Judah, and despite the warnings of noble and eloquent prophets she perished. It is now a good many years since Mr. Arnold cited Isaiah and Plato for our benefit to illustrate his belief that with us, as with Judah and Athens, the majority are unsound. And yet from his essay on Numbers — an essay for which Lowell's " Democracy " is an excellent antidote — we may turn with a feeling of confidence and security to that un- tired and unwearying majority which Arnold believed to be unsound. Many instances of the soundness of our majority have been afforded

The Tired Business Man

since Mr. Arnold's death, and it is a reasonable expectation that, in spite of the apparent ease with which the majority may be stampeded, it nevertheless pauses with a safe margin between it and the precipice. Illustrations of failure abound in history, but the very rise and development of our nation has discredited History as a prophet. In the multiplication of big and little Smiths lies our only serious danger. The disposition of the sick Smiths to deplore as unhealthy and unsound such a radical movement as began in 1896, and still sweeps merrily on in 1912, never seriously arrests the onward march of those who sincerely believe that we were meant to be a great refuge for mankind. If I must choose, I prefer to take my chances with the earnest, healthy, patriotic millions rather than with an oligarchy of tired Smiths. Our impatience of the bounds of law set by men who died before the Republic was born does not justify the whimpering of those Smiths who wrap themselves in the grave-clothes of old precedents, and who love the Constitution only when they fly to it for shelter. Tired business men, weary professional

men, bored farmers, timorous statesmen are
not of the vigorous stuff of those

> "Who founded us and spread from sea to sea
> A thousand leagues the zone of liberty,
> And gave to man this refuge from his past,
> Unkinged, unchurched, unsoldiered."

Our country's only enemies are the sick men,
the tired men, who have exhausted themselves
in the vain pursuit of vain things; who forget
that democracy like Christianity is essentially
social, and who constitute a sick remnant from
whom it is devoutly to be hoped the benign
powers may forever protect us.

VII

It was a year ago that I met my old friend
Smith, irritable, depressed, anxious, in the German capital. This morning we tramped five
miles, here among the Vermont hills where he
has established himself. Sound in wind and
limb is my old neighbor, and his outlook on life
is sane and reasonable. I have even heard him
referring, with something of his old emotion, to
that dark winter at Valley Forge, but with a
new hopefulness, a wider vision. He does not

The Tired Business Man

think the American Republic will perish, even as Nineveh and Tyre, any more than I do. He has come to a realization of his own errors and he is interested in the contemplation of his own responsibilities. And it is not the German specialist he has to thank for curing his weariness half so much as Fanny.

Fanny! Fanny is the wisest, the most capable, the healthiest-minded girl in the world. Fanny is adorable! As we trudged along the road, Smith suddenly paused and lifted his eyes to a rough pasture slightly above and beyond us. I knew from the sudden light in his face that Fanny was in the landscape. She leaped upon a wall and waved to us. A cool breeze rose from the valley and swept round her. As she poised for a moment before running down to join us in the road, there was about her something of the grace and vigor of the Winged Victory as it challenges the eye at the head of the staircase in the Louvre. She lifted her hand to brush back her hair, — that golden crown so loved by light! And as she ran we knew she would neither stumble nor fall on that rock-strewn pasture. When she reached the brook she took it at a bound, and burst upon us radiant.

It had been Fanny's idea to come here, and poor, tired, broken, disconsolate Smith, driven desperate by the restrictions imposed upon him by the German doctors, and only harassed by his wife's fears, had yielded to Fanny's importunities. I had been so drawn into their affairs that I knew all the steps by which Fanny had effected his redemption. She had broken through the lines of the Philistines and brought him a cup of water from that unquenchable well by the gate for which David pined and for which we all long when the evil days come. The youth of a world that never grows old is in Fanny's heart. She is to Smith as a Goddess of Liberty in short skirt and sweater, come down from her pedestal to lead the way to green pastures beside waters of comfort. She has become to him not merely the spirit of youth but of life, and his dependence upon her is complete. It was she who saved him from himself when to his tired eyes it seemed that

"All one's work is vain,
And life goes stretching on, a waste gray plain,

184

The Tired Business Man

With even the short mirage of morning gone,
No cool breath anywhere, no shadow nigh
Where a weary man might lay him down and die."

Later, as we sat on Smith's veranda watching
the silver trumpet of the young moon beyond the pine-crowned crest, with the herd a
dark blur in the intervening meadows, and
sweet clean airs blowing out of the valley, it
somehow occurred to me that Fanny of the
adorable head, Fanny gentle of heart, quick
of wit, and ready of hand, is the fine essence
of all that is worthiest and noblest in this
America of ours. In such as she there is both
inspiration to do and the wisdom of peace and
rest. As she sits brooding with calm brows, a
quiet hand against her tanned cheek, I see in
her the likeness of a goddess sprung of loftier
lineage than Olympus knew, for in her abides
the spirit of that old and new America that
labors in the sun and whose faith is in the stars.

The Spirit of Mischief:
A Dialogue

The Spirit of Mischief:
A Dialogue

If I could find a higher tree
Farther and farther I should see,
To where the grown-up river slips
Into the sea among the ships.

To where the roads on either hand
Lead onward into fairyland,
Where all the children dine at five,
And all the playthings come alive.

R. L. S.

JESSAMINE and I had been out sailing. We
came back to find the house deserted,
and after foraging in the pantry, we made
ourselves at home in the long unceiled living-
room, which is one of the pleasantest lounging-
places in the world. A few pine-knots were
smouldering in the fireplace, and, as I have
reached an age when it is pleasant to watch
the flames, I poked a little life into the embers
and sat down to contemplate them from the
easiest chair the camp afforded. Jessamine

wearily cast herself upon the couch near by without taking off her coat.

Jessamine is five and does as she likes, and does it perversely, arbitrarily, and gracefully, in the way of maids of five. In the pantry she had found her way to marmalade with an ease and certainty that amazed me; and she had, with malice aforethought, made me *particeps criminis* by teaching me how to coax reluctant, tight-fitting olives from an impossible bottle with an oyster-fork.

Jessamine is difficult. I thought of it now with a pang, as her brown curls lay soft against a red cushion and she crunched a biscuit, heavily stuccoed with marmalade, with her little popcorn teeth. I have wooed her with bonbons; I have bribed her with pennies; but indifference and disdain are still my portion. To-day was my opportunity. The rest of the household had gone to explore the village bazaars, and we were left alone. It was not that she loved me more, but the new nurse less; and, as sailing had usually been denied her, she derived from our few hours in my catboat the joy of a clandestine adventure. We had never been so much to-

The Spirit of Mischief

gether before. I wondered how long the spell of our sail would last. Probably, I reflected, until the wanderers came back from town to afford a new diversion; or until her nurse came to carry her away to tea. For the moment, however, I felt secure. The fire snapped; the clock ticked insistently; my face burned from its recent contact with a sharp west wind, which had brought white caps to the surface of the lake and a pleasant splash to the beach at our front door. Jessamine folded her arms, rested her head upon them, and regarded me lazily. She was slim and lean of limb, and the lines she made on the couch were long. I tried to remember whether I had ever seen her still before.

"You may read, if you like," she said.

"Thank you; but I'd rather have you tell me things," I answered.

I wished to be conciliatory. At any moment, I knew she might rise and vanish. My tricks of detention had proved futile a thousand times; I was always losing her. She was a master opportunist. She had, I calculated, a mood a minute, and the mood of inaction was not often one of them.

The Spirit of Mischief

"There are many, many things I'd like to have you tell me, Mischief," I said. "What do you think of when you're all alone; what do you think of me?"

"Oh! I never think of you when I'm all alone."

"Thank you, Mischief. But I wonder whether you are quite frank. You must think of me sometimes. For example, — where were you when you thought of knotting my neckties all together, no longer ago than yesterday?"

"Oh!" (It is thus she begins many sentences. Her "Ohs" are delightfully equivocal.)

"Perhaps you'd rather not tell. Of course, I don't mind about the ties."

"It was nice of you — not to mind."

Suddenly her blue eyes ceased to be. They are little pools of blue, like mountain lakes. I was aware that the dark lashes had stolen down upon her brown cheek. She opened her eyes again instantly.

"I wish I hadn't found your ties. Finding them made a lot of trouble for me. I was looking for your funny little scissors to open the door of my doll-house that was stuck, and I saw

192

The Spirit of Mischief

the ties. Then I remembered that I needed a rope to tie Adolphus — that's the woolly dog you bought for my birthday — to my bed at night; and neckties make very good ropes."

"I'm glad to hear it, Mischief."

"There's a prayer they say in church about mischief — " she began sleepily.

"'From all evil and mischief; from sin; from the crafts and assaults of the Devil?'" I quoted.

"That is it! and there's something in it, too, about everlasting damnation, that always sends shivers down my back."

She frowned in a puzzled way. I remembered that once, when Jessamine and I went to church together, she had, during the reading of the litany, so moved a silk hat on the next seat that its owner crushed it hideously when he rose from his knees.

The black lashes hid the blue eyes once more, and she settled her head snugly into her folded arms.

"Why," she murmured, "do you call me Mischief? I'm not Mischief; I'm Jessamine."

"You are the Spirit of Mischief," I answered; and she made no reply.

The Spirit of Mischief

The water of the lake beat the shore stormily.

"The Spirit of Mischief."

Jessamine repeated the words sleepily. I had never thought of them seriously before, and had applied them to her thoughtlessly. Is there, I asked myself, a whimsical spirit that possesses the heart of a child, — something that is too swift for the slow pace of adult minds; and if there be such, where is its abiding-place?

"I'm the Spirit of Mischief!"

There, with her back to the fire, stood Jessamine, but with a difference. Her fists were thrust deep down into the pockets of her coat. There was a smile on her face that I did not remember to have seen before. The wind had blown her hair into a sorry tangle, and it was my fault — I should have made her wear her tam-o'-shanter in the catboat! An uncle may mean well, but, after all, he is no fit substitute for a parent.

"So you admit it, do you? It is unlike you to make concessions."

"You use long words. Uncles *always* use long words. It is one of the most foolish things they do."

194

The Spirit of Mischief

"I'm sorry. I wish very much not to be foolish or naughty."

"I have wished that many times," she returned gravely. "But naughtiness and mischief are not the same thing."

"I believe that is so," I answered. "But if you are really the Spirit of Mischief, — and far be it from me to doubt your word, — where is your abiding-place? Spirits must have abiding-places."

"There are many of them, and they are a long way off. One is where the four winds meet."

"But that — that isn't telling. Nobody knows where that is."

"Everybody doesn't," said the Spirit of Mischief gently, as one who would deal forbearingly with dullness.

"Tell me something easier," I begged.

"Well, I'll try again," she said. "Sometimes when I'm not where four winds meet, I'm at the end of all the rainbows. Do you know that place?"

"I never heard of it. Is it very far away?"

"It's farther than anything — farther even than the place where the winds meet."

195

The Spirit of Mischief

"And what do you do there? You must have bags and bags of gold, O Spirit."

"Yes. Of course. I practice hiding things with them. That is why no one ever found a bag of gold at the end of a rainbow. I have put countless ones in the cave of lost treasure. There are a great many things there besides the bags of gold, — things that parents, and uncles, and aunts lose, — and never find any more."

"I wish I could visit the place," I said with a sigh. "It would be pleasant to see a storehouse like that. It would have, I may say, a strong personal interest. Only yesterday I contributed a valued scarf-pin through the agency of a certain mischievous niece; and I shall be long in recovering from the loss of that miraculous putter that made me a terror on the links. My golf can never be the same again."

"But you never can see the place," she declared. "A time comes when you can't find it any more, the cave of lost treasure — or the place where four winds meet — or the end of all the rainbows."

"I suppose I have lost my chance," I said.

The Spirit of Mischief

"Oh, long ago!" exclaimed the Spirit disdainfully. "It never lasts beyond six!"

"That has a wise sound. Pray tell me more! Tell me, I beg, how you have endured this harsh world so long."

This, I thought, was a poser; but she answered readily enough.

"I suppose, because I am kindred of so many, many things that live on forever. There are the colors on water when the sun strikes it through clouds. It can be green and gold and blue and silver all at once; and then there is the foam of the white caps. It is foam for a moment and then it is just water again. And there is the moonlight on rippling water, that goes away and never comes any more — not just the same. The mirth in the heart of a child is like all these things; and the heart of a child is the place I love best."

"Yes," I said. "I'm sure it is better than the place where all the winds meet, or that other rainbow-place that you told me about."

"And then," she began again, "you know that children say things sometimes just in fun, but no one ever seems to understand that."

The Spirit of Mischief

"To be sure," I said feelingly, remembering how Jessamine loved to tease and plague me.

"But there is n't any harm in it — any more than —"

"Yes?" a little impatiently.

"Than in the things the pines say when the wind runs over the top of them. They are not — not important, exactly, — but they are always different. That is the best thing about being a child — the being different part. You have a grown-up word that means always just the same."

"Consistent?" I asked.

"That is it. A child that is consistent is wrong some way. But I don't remember having seen any of that kind."

A smile that was not the smile of Jessamine stole into the Spirit's face. It disconcerted me. I could not, for the life of me, decide how much of the figure before me was Jessamine and how much was really the Spirit of Mischief, or whether they were both the same.

"Being ignorant, you don't know what the mirth in a child is — you" (scornfully) "who

The Spirit of Mischief

pretend to measure all people by their sense of humor. It's akin to the bubbling music of the fountain of youth, and you do the child and the world a wrong when you stifle it. A child's glee is as natural as sunshine, and carries no burden of knowledge; and that is the precious thing about it."

"I'm sure that is true," I said; but the Spirit did not heed me. She went on, in a voice that suggested Jessamine, but was not hers.

"Many people talk solemnly about the imagination of children, as though it were a thing that could be taught from books or prepared in laboratories. But children's mischief, that is so often complained of, is the imaginations' finest flower."

"The idea pleases me. I shall make a note of it."

"The very day," continued the Spirit, "that you sat at table and talked learnedly about the minds of children and how to promote in them a love of the beautiful, your Jessamine had known a moment of joy. She had lain in the meadow and watched the thistledown take flight, — a myriad of those flimsy argosies.

The Spirit of Mischief

And she had fashioned a story about them, that they rise skyward to become the stuff that white clouds are made of. And the same day she asked you to tell her what it is the robins are so sorry about when they sing in the evening after the other birds have gone. Now the same small head that thought of those things contrived also the happy idea of cooking a doll's dinner in the chafing dish, — an experiment that resulted, as you may remember, in a visit from both the doctor and the fire-insurance adjuster."

My heart was wrung as I recalled the bandages on Jessamine's slender brown arms.

"Yes, O Spirit!" I said. "I'm learning much. Pray tell me more!"

"We like very much for science to let us alone —"

"But hygiene — and all those life-saving things —"

"Oh, yes," she said patronizingly; "they're all very well in their way. It's better for science to kill bugs than for the bugs to kill children. But I mean other kinds of sciences that are not nearly so useful — pedagogical and the like,

The Spirit of Mischief

that are trying to kill the microbe of play. Leave us, oh, leave us that!"

"That is a new way of putting it. We oldsters soon forget how to play, alackaday!"

She went on calmly. "Work that you really love is n't work any more — it's play."

"That's a little deep for me —"

"It's true, though, so you'd better try to understand. If you paint a picture and work at it, — slave over it and are not happy doing it, — then your picture is only so many pennies' worth of paint. The cruelest thing people can say of a book or a picture is, 'Well, he worked hard at it!' The spirit of mischief is only the spirit of play; and the spirit of play is really the spirit of the work we love."

"It's too bad that you are not always patient with us," the Spirit continued. (I noted the plural. Clearly Jessamine and the Spirit were one!)

"I'm sorry, too," I answered contritely.

"The laws of the foolish world do not apply to childhood at all. Children are born into a condition of ideality. They view everything with wonder and awe, and you and all the rest

The Spirit of Mischief

of the grown-up world are busy spoiling their illusions. How happy you would be if you could have gone on blowing bubbles all your days!"

"True, alas, too true!"

The face of the Spirit grew suddenly very old.

"Life," she said, "consists largely in having to accept the fact that we cannot do the things we want to do. But in the blessed days of mischief we blow bubbles in forbidden soap and water with contraband pipes — and do not know that they are bubbles!"

"That is the fine thing about it, O Spirit — the sweet ignorance of it! I hope I understand that."

"I see that you are really wiser than you have always seemed," she said, with her baffling smile. "Mischief, as you are prone to call so many things that children do, is as wholesome and sweet as a field of clover. I, the Spirit of Mischief, have a serious business in the world, which I'll tell you about, as you are old and know so little. I'm here to combat and confuse the evil spirits that seek to stifle the good cheer of childhood. These little children that always go to bed without a fuss and say good night

The Spirit of Mischief

very sweetly in French, and never know bread and butter and jam by their real names — you really do not like them half as well as you like natural children. You remember that you laughed when Jessamine's French governess came, and left the second day because the black cat got into her trunk. There was really no harm in that!"

The Spirit of Mischief laughed. She grew very small, and I watched her curiously, wondering whether she was really a creature of this work-a-day world. Then suddenly she grew to life-size again, and laughed gleefully, standing with her hands thrust deep into her coat pockets.

"Jessamine!" I exclaimed. "I thought you were asleep."

"I was, a little bit; but you — you snored awfully," she said, "and waked me up."

She still watched me, laughing; and looking down I saw that she had been busy while I slept. A barricade of books had been built around me, — a carefully wrought bit of masonry, as high as my knees.

"You're the wicked giant," declared Jessamine, quite in her own manner, and with no

The Spirit of Mischief

hint of the half-real, elfish spirit of my dream. "And I'm the good little Princess that has caught you at last. And I'll never let you out of the tower — Oh they're coming! They're coming!"

She flashed to the door and out upon the veranda where steps had sounded, leaving me to deliver myself from the tower of the Spirit of Mischief with the ignorant hands of Age.

Confessions of a "Best-Seller"

Confessions of a "Best-Seller"

THAT my name has adorned best-selling lists is more of a joke than my harshest critics can imagine. I had dallied awhile at the law; I had given ten full years to journalism; I had written criticism, and not a little verse; two or three short stories of the slightest had been my only adventure in fiction; and I had spent a year writing an essay in history, which, from the publisher's reports, no one but my neighbor and my neighbor's wife ever read. My frugal output of poems had pleased no one half so much as myself; and having reached years of discretion I carefully analyzed samples of the ore that remained in my bins, decided that I had exhausted my poetical vein, and thereupon turned rather soberly to the field of fiction.

In order to qualify myself to speak to my text, I will say that in a period of six years, that closed in January, 1909, my titles were included

Confessions of a Best-Seller

fifteen times in the "Bookman" list of best-selling books. Two of my titles appeared five times each; one of them headed the list three months successively. I do not presume to speak for others with whom I have crossed swords in the best-selling lists, but I beg to express my strong conviction that the compilation of such statistics is quite as injurious as it is helpful to authors. When the "six best-selling" phrase was new the monthly statement of winners may have carried some weight; but for several years it has really had little significance. Critical purchasers are likely to be wary of books so listed. It is my impression, based on talks with retail dealers in many parts of the country, that they often report as "best-sellers" books of which they may have made large advance purchases, but which are selling slowly. Their aim is, of course, to force the book into the list, and thereby create a false impression of its popularity.

I think that most publishers, and many authors who, like myself, have profited by the making of these lists, would gladly see them discontinued. The fact remains, however, that

Confessions of a Best-Seller

the best novels by the best English and American writers have generally been included in these lists. Mrs. Wharton, Mrs. Ward, Mr. Winston Churchill, Mr. Wister, "Kate Douglas Wiggin," Miss Johnston, and Mr. William de Morgan have, for example, shared with inferior writers the ignominy of popular success. I do not believe that my American fellow citizens prefer trash to sound literature. There are not enough novels of the first order, not enough books of the style and solidity of "The House of Mirth" and "Joseph Vance," to satisfy the popular demand for fiction; and while the people wait, they take inferior books, like several bearing my own name, which have no aim but to amuse. I know of nothing more encouraging to those who wish to see the American novel go high and far than the immediate acceptance among us of the writings of Mr. William de Morgan, who makes no concession, not even of brevity, to the ever-increasing demand for fiction.

I spent the greater part of two years on my first novel, which dealt with aspects of life in an urban community which interested me; and the gravest fault of the book, if I am entitled to an opinion, is its self-consciousness, — I was too anxious, too painstaking, with the result that those pages seem frightfully stiff to me now. The book was launched auspiciously; my publisher advertised it generously, and it landed safely among the "six best-sellers." The critical reception of the book was cordial and friendly, not only in the newspaper press, but in the more cautious weekly journals. My severest critic dealt far more amiably with my book than I should have done myself, if I had sat in judgment upon it. I have been surprised to find the book still remembered, and its quality has been flung in my face by critics who have deplored my later performances.

I now wrote another novel, to which I gave even greater care, and into it I put, I think, the best characterizations I have ever done; but the *soupçon* of melodrama with which I flavored the first novel was lacking in the second, and it went dead a little short of fifteen thousand — the poorest sale any of my books has had.

A number of my friends were, at this time,

Confessions of a Best-Seller

rather annoyingly directing my attention to the
great popular successes of several other American writers, whose tales were, I felt, the most
contemptible *pastiche*, without the slightest
pretense to originality, and having neither form
nor style. It was in some bitterness of spirit
that I resolved to try my hand at a story that
should be a story and nothing else. Nor should
I storm the capitals of imaginary kingdoms, but
set the scene on my own soil. Most, it was clear,
could grow the flowers of Zenda when once the
seed had been scattered by Mr. Hawkins.
Whether Mr. Hawkins got his inspiration from
the flora of Prince Otto's gardens, and whether
the Prince was indebted in his turn to Harry
Richmond, is not my affair. I am, no doubt,
indebted to all three of these creations; but
I set my scene in an American commonwealth,
a spot that derived nothing from historical association, and sent my hero on his adventures
armed with nothing more deadly than a suit-
case and an umbrella. The idea is not original
with me that you can make anything interesting if you know how. It was Stevenson, I believe, who said that a kitchen table is a fair

Confessions of a Best-Seller

enough subject for any writer who knows his trade. I do not cite myself as a person capable of proving this; but I am satisfied that the chief fun of story-telling lies in trying, by all the means in a writer's power, to make plausible the seemingly impossible. And here, of course, I am referring to the story for the story's sake, — not to the novel of life and manners.

My two earliest books were clearly too deliberate. They were deficient in incident, and I was prone to wander into blind alleys, and not always ingenious enough to emerge again upon the main thoroughfare. I felt that, while I might fail in my attempt to produce a romantic yarn, the experience might help me to a better understanding of the mechanics of the novel, — that I might gain directness, movement, and ease.

For my third venture I hit upon a device that took strong hold upon my imagination. The idea of laying a trap for the reader tickled me; and when once I had written the first chapter and outlined the last, I yielded myself to the story and bade it run its own course. I was never more honestly astonished in my life than

Confessions of a Best-Seller

to find my half-dozen characters taking matters into their own hands, and leaving me the merest spectator and reporter. I had made notes for the story, but in looking them over to-day, I find that I made practically no use of them. I never expect to experience again the delight of the winter I spent over that tale. The sight of white paper had no terrors for me. The hero, constantly cornered, had always in his pocket the key to his successive dilemmas; the heroine, misunderstood and misjudged, was struck at proper intervals by the spot-light that revealed her charm and reëstablished faith in her honorable motives. No other girl in my little gallery of heroines exerts upon me the spell of that young lady, who, on the day I began the story, as I waited for the ink to thaw in my workshop, passed under my window, by one of those kindly orderings of Providence that keep alive the superstition of inspiration in the hearts of all fiction-writers. She never came my way again — but she need not! She was the bright particular star of my stage — its *dea ex machina*. She is of the sisterhood of radiant goddesses who are visible from any window, even

Confessions of a Best-Seller

though its prospect be only a commonplace city
street. Always, and everywhere, the essential
woman for any tale is passing by with grave
mien, if the tale be sober; with upturned chin
and a saucy twinkle in the eye, if such be the
seeker's need!

I think I must have begun every morning's
work with a grin on my face, for it was all fun,
and I entered with zest into all the changes and
chances of the story. I was embarrassed, not
by any paucity of incident, but by my own
fecundity and dexterity. The audacity of my
project used sometimes to give me pause; it was
almost too bold a thing to carry through; but
my curiosity as to just how the ultimate goal
would be reached kept my interest keyed high.
At times, feeling that I was going too fast, I
used to halt and write a purple patch or two
for my own satisfaction, — a harmless diversion to which I am prone, and which no one
could be cruel enough to deny me. There are
pages in that book over which I dallied for a
week, and in looking at them now I find that
I still think them— as Mr. James would say —
"rather nice." And once, while thus amusing

myself, a phrase slipped from the pen which I saw at once had been, from all time, ordained to be the title of my book.

When I had completed the first draft, I began retouching. I liked my tale so much that I was reluctant to part with it; I enjoyed playing with it, and I think I rewrote the most of it three times. Contumelious critics have spoken of me as one of the typewriter school of fictionists, picturing me as lightly flinging off a few chapters before breakfast, and spending the rest of the day on the golf-links; but I have never in my life written in a first draft more than a thousand words a day, and I have frequently thrown away a day's work when I came to look it over. I have refused enough offers for short stories, serials, and book rights, to have kept half a dozen typewriters busy, and my output has not been large, considering that writing has been, for nearly ten years, my only occupation. I can say, with my hand on my heart, that I have written for my own pleasure first and last, and that those of my books that have enjoyed the greatest popularity were written really in a spirit of play, without any

illusions as to their importance or their quick
and final passing into the void.

When I had finished my story, I still had a
few incidents and scenes in my ink-pot; but I
could not for the life of me get the curtain up,
once it was down. My little drama had put itself together as tight as wax, and even when I
had written an additional incident that pleased
me particularly, I could find no place to thrust
it in. I was interested chiefly in amusing myself, and I never troubled myself in the least as
to whether anyone else would care for the story.
I was astonished by its sale, which exceeded a
quarter of a million copies in this country; it
has been translated into French, Italian, German, Danish, Swedish, and Norwegian. I have
heard of it all the way from Tokyo to Teheran.
It was dramatized, and an actor of distinction
appeared in the stage version; and stock companies have lately presented the play in Boston
and San Francisco. It was subsequently serial-
ized by newspapers, and later appeared in
"patent" supplements. The title was para-
phrased by advertisers, several of whom continue to pay me this flattering tribute.

Confessions of a Best-Seller

I have speculated a good deal as to the success of this book. The title had, no doubt, much to do with it; clever advertising helped it further; the cover was a lure to the eye. The name of a popular illustrator may have helped, but it is certain that his pictures did not! I think I am safe in saying that the book received no helpful reviews in any newspapers of the first class, and I may add that I am skeptical as to the value of favorable notices in stimulating the sale of such books. Serious novels are undoubtedly helped by favorable reviews; stories of the kind I describe depend primarily upon persistent and ingenious advertising, in which a single striking line from the "Gem City Evening Gazette" is just as valuable as the opinion of the most scholarly review. Nor am I unmindful of the publisher's labors and risks, — the courage, confidence, and genius essential to a successful campaign with a book from a new hand, with no prestige of established reputation to command instant recognition. The self-selling book may become a "best-seller"; it may appear mysteriously, a "dark horse" ir the eternal battle of the books; but miracles are

Confessions of a Best-Seller

as rare in the book trade as in other lines of commerce. The man behind the counter is another important factor. The retail dealer, when he finds the publisher supporting him with advertising, can do much to prolong a sale. A publisher of long experience in promoting large sales has told me that advertising is valuable chiefly for its moral effect on the retailer, who, feeling that the publisher is strongly backing a book, bends his own energies toward keeping it alive.

It would be absurd for me to pretend that the leap from a mild *succès d'estime* with sales of forty and fourteen thousand, to a delirious gallop into six figures is not without its effect on an author, unless he be much less human than I am. Those gentle friends who had intimated that I could not do it once, were equally sanguine that I could not do it again. The temptation to try a second throw of the dice after a success is strong, but I debated long whether I should try my hand at a second romance. I resolved finally to do a better book in the same kind, and with even more labor I produced a yarn whose title — and the gods have several

times favored me in the matter of titles —
adorned the best-selling lists for an even
longer period, though the total sales aggregated
less.

The second romance was, I think, better than
the first, and its dramatic situations were more
picturesque. The reviews averaged better in
better places, and may have aroused the prejudices of those who shun books that are counte-
nanced or praised by the literary "high brows."
It sold largely; it enjoyed the glory and the
shame of a "best-seller"; but here, I pondered, was the time to quit. Not to shock my
"audience," to use the term of the trade, I
resolved to try for more solid ground by paying
more attention to characterizations, and cut-
ting down the allowance of blood and thunder.
I expected to lose heavily with the public, and
I was not disappointed. I crept into the best-
selling list, but my sojourn there was brief. It
is manifest that people who like shots in the
dark will not tamely acquiesce in the mild placing of the villain's hand upon his hip pocket on
the moon-washed terrace. The difference between the actual shot and the mere menace, I

could, from personal knowledge, compute in the coin of the Republic.

When your name on the bill-board suggests battle, murder, and sudden death, "hair-breadth 'scapes, i' th' imminent deadly breach," and that sort of thing, you need not be chagrined if, once inside, the eager throng resents bitterly your perfidy in offering nothing more blood-curdling than the heroine's demand (the scene being set for five o'clock tea) for another lump of sugar. You may, if you please, leave Hamlet out of his own play; but do not, on peril of your fame, cut out your ghost, or neglect to provide some one to stick a sword into Polonius behind the arras. I can take up that particular book now and prove to any fair-minded man how prettily I could, by injecting a little paprika into my villains, have quadrupled its sale.

Having, I hope, some sense of humor, I resolved to bid farewell to cloak and pistols in a farce-comedy, which should be a take-off on my own popular performances. Humor being something that no one should tamper with who is not ready for the gibbet, I was not surprised

Confessions of a Best-Seller

that many hasty samplers of the book should entirely miss the joke, or that a number of joyless critics should have dismissed it hastily as merely another machine-made romance written for boarding-school girls and the weary commercial traveler yawning in the smoking-car. Yet this book also has been a "best-seller"! I have seen it, within a few weeks, prominently displayed in bookshop windows in half a dozen cities.

It was, I think, Mr. Clyde Fitch who first voiced the complaint that our drama is seriously affected by the demand of "the tired business man" to be amused at the theatre. The same may be said of fiction. A very considerable number of our toiling millions sit down wearily at night, and if the evening paper does not fully satisfy or social diversion offer, a story that will hold the attention without too great a tax upon the mind is welcomed. I should be happy to think that our ninety millions trim the lamp every evening with zest for "improving" literature; but the tired brain follows the line of least resistance, which unfortunately does not lead to alcoves where the

Confessions of a Best-Seller

one hundred best books wear their purple in solemn pomp. Even in my present mood of contrition, I am not sneering at that considerable body of my countrymen who have laid one dollar and eighteen cents upon the counter and borne home my little fictions. They took grave chances of my boring them; and when they rapped a second time on the counter and murmured another of my titles, they were expressing a confidence in me which I strove hard never to betray.

No one will, I am sure, deny me the satisfaction I have in the reflection that I put a good deal of sincere work into those stories, — for they are stories, not novels, and were written frankly to entertain; that they are not wholly ill-written; that they contain pages that are not without their grace; or that there is nothing prurient or morbid in any of them. And no matter how jejune stories of the popular romantic type may be, — a fact, O haughty critic, of which I am well aware, — I take some satisfaction as a good American in the knowledge that, in spite of their worthlessness as literature, they are essentially clean. The

Confessions of a Best-Seller

heroes may be too handsome, and too sure of themselves; the heroines too adorable in their sweet distress, as they wave the white handkerchief from the grated window of the ivied tower, — but their adventures are, in the very nature of things, *in usum Delphini.*

Some of my friends of the writing guild boast that they never read criticisms of their work. I have read and filed all the notices of my stories that bore any marks of honesty or intelligence. Having served my own day as reviewer for a newspaper, I know the dreary drudgery of such work. I recall, with shame, having averaged a dozen books an afternoon; and some of my critics have clearly averaged two dozen, with my poor candidates for oblivion at the bottom of the heap! Much American criticism is stupid or ignorant; but the most depressing, from my standpoint, is the flippant sort of thing which many newspapers print habitually. The stage, also, suffers like treatment, even in some of the more reputable metropolitan journals. Unless your book affords a text for a cynical newspaper "story," it is quite likely to be ignored.

I cannot imagine that any writer who takes

Confessions of a Best-Seller

his calling seriously ever resents a sincere, intelligent, adverse notice. I have never written a book in less than a year, devoting all my time to it; and I resent being dismissed in a line, and called a writer of drivel, by some one who did not take the trouble to say why. A newspaper which is particularly jealous of its good name once pointed out with elaborate care that an incident, described in one of my stories as occurring in broad daylight, could not have been observed in moonlight by one of the characters at the distance I had indicated. The same reviewer transferred the scene of this story halfway across the continent, in order to make another point against its plausibility. If the aim of criticism be to aid the public in its choice of books, then the press should deal fairly with both author and public. And if the critics wish to point out to authors their failures and weaknesses, then it should be done in a spirit of justice. The best-selling of my books caused a number of critics to remark that it had clearly been inspired by a number of old romances — which I had not only never read, but of several of them I had never even heard.

Confessions of a Best-Seller

A Boston newspaper which I greatly admire once published an editorial in which I was pilloried as a type of writer who basely commercializes his talent. It was a cruel stab; for, unlike my heroes, I do not wear a mail-shirt under my dress-coat. Once, wandering into a church in my own city, at a time when a dramatized version of one of my stories was offered at a local theatre, I listened to a sermon that dealt in the harshest terms with such fiction and drama.

Extravagant or ignorant praise is, to most of us, as disheartening as stupid and unjust criticism. The common practice of invoking great names to praise some new arrival at the portal of fame cannot fail to depress the subject of it. When my first venture in fiction was flatteringly spoken of by a journal which takes its criticisms seriously as evidencing the qualities that distinguish Mr. Howells, I shuddered at the hideous injustice to a gentleman for whom I have the greatest love and reverence; and when, in my subsequent experiments, a critic somewhere gravely (it seemed, at least, to be in a spirit of sobriety!) asked whether a fold of

Confessions of a Best-Seller

Stevenson's mantle had not wrapped itself about me, the awfulness of the thing made me ill, and I fled from felicity until my publisher had dropped the heart-breaking phrase from his advertisements. For I may be the worst living author, and at times I am convinced of it; but I hope I am not an immitigable and irreclaimable ass.

American book reviewers, I am convinced from a study of my returns from the clipping bureaus for ten years, dealing with my offerings in two kinds of fiction, are a solid phalanx of realists where they are anything at all. This attitude is due, I imagine, to the fact that journalism deals, or is supposed to deal, with facts. Realism is certainly more favorably received than romance. I cheerfully subscribe to the doctrine that fiction that lays strong hands upon aspects of life as we are living it is a nobler achievement than tales that provide merely an evening's entertainment. Mr. James has, however, simplified this whole question. He says, "The only classification of the novel that I can understand is into that which has life, and that which has it not"; and if we must reduce this matter of fiction to law, his dictum might well be accepted as the first and last canon. And in this connection I should like to record my increasing admiration for all that Mr. James has written of novels and novelists. In one place and another he has expressed himself fully and confidently on fiction as a department of literature. The lecture on Balzac that he gave in this country a few years ago is a masterly and authoritative document on the novel in general. His "Partial Portraits" is a rich mine of ripe observation on the distinguishing qualities of a number of his contemporaries, and the same volume contains a suggestive and stimulating essay on fiction as an art. With these in mind it seems to me a matter for tears that Mr. James, with his splendid equipment and beautiful genius, should have devoted himself so sedulously, in his own performances in fiction, to the contemplation of cramped foreign vistas and exotic types, when all this wide, surging, eager, laboring America lay ready to his hand.

I will say of myself that I value style beyond most things; and that if I could command

Confessions of a Best-Seller

it, I should be glad to write for so small an
audience, the "fit though few," that the best-
selling lists should never know me again; for
with style go many of the requisites of great
fiction, — fineness and sureness of feeling, and a
power over language by which characters cease
to be bobbing marionettes and become veritable
beings, no matter whether they are Beatrix
Esmonds, or strutting D'Artagnans, or rascally
Bartley Hubbards, or luckless Lily Barts. To
toss a ball into the air, and keep it there, as
Stevenson did so charmingly in such pieces as
"Providence and the Guitar," — this is a
respectable achievement; to mount Roy Richmond as an equestrian statue, — that, too, is
something we would not have had Mr. Meredith leave undone. Mr. Rassendyll, an English
gentleman playing at being king, thrills the
surviving drop of mediævalism that is in all of
us. "The tired business man" yields himself to
the belief that the staccato of hoofs on the
asphalt street, which steals in to him faintly at
his fireside, is really an accompaniment to the
hero's mad ride to save the king. Ah, the joy
in kings dies hard in us!

Confessions of a Best-Seller

Given a sprightly tale with a lost message to recover, throw in a fight on the stair, scatter here and there pretty dialogues between the lover and the princess he serves, and we are all, as we breathlessly follow, the rankest royalists. Tales of real Americans, kodaked "in the sun's hot eye," much as they refresh me, — I speak of myself now, not as a writer or critic, but as the man in the street, — never so completely detach the weary spirit from mundane things as tales of events that never were on sea or land. Why should I read of Silas Lapham to-night, when only an hour ago I was his competitor in the mineral-paint business? The greatest fiction must be a criticism of life; but there are times when we crave forgetfulness, and lift our eyes trustfully to the flag of Zenda.

But the creator of Zenda, it is whispered, is not an author of the first or even of the second rank, and the adventure story, at its best, is only for the second table. I am quite aware of this. But pause a moment, O cheerless one! Surely Homer is respectable; and the Iliad, the most strenuous, the most glorious and sublime of fictions, with the very gods drawn into the

Confessions of a Best-Seller

moving scenes, has, by reason of its tremendous
energy and its tumultuous drama, not less than
for its majesty as literature, established its
right to be called the longest-selling fiction of
the ages.

All the world loves a story; the regret is that
the great novelists — great in penetration and
sincerity and style — do not always have the
story-telling knack. Mr. Marion Crawford
was, I should say, a far better story-teller than
Mr. James or Mr. Howells; but I should by no
means call him a better novelist. A lady of my
acquaintance makes a point of bestowing copies
of Mr. Meredith's novels upon young working-
women whom she seeks to uplift. I am myself
the most ardent of Meredithians, and yet I
must confess to a lack of sympathy with this
lady's high purpose. I will not press the point,
but a tired working-girl would, I think, be much
happier with one of my own beribboned con-
fections than with even Diana the delectable.

Pleasant it is, I must confess, to hear your
wares cried by the train-boy; to bend a sympathetic ear to his recital of your merits, as he
appraises them; and to watch him beguile your

Confessions of a Best-Seller

fellow travelers with the promise of felicity contained between the covers of the book which you yourself have devised, pondered, and committed to paper. The train-boy's ideas of the essentials of entertaining fiction are radically unacademic, but he is apt in hitting off the commercial requirements. A good book, one of the guild told me, should always begin with "talking." He was particularly contemptuous of novels that open upon landscape and moonlight, — these, in the bright lexicon of his youthful experience, are well-nigh unsalable. And he was equally scornful of the unhappy ending. The sale of a book that did not, as he put it, "come out right," that is, with the merry jingle of wedding-bells, was no less than a fraud upon the purchaser. On one well-remembered occasion my vanity was gorged by the sight of many copies of my latest offering in the hands of my fellow travelers, as I sped from Washington to New York. A poster, announcing my new tale, greeted me at the station as I took flight; four copies of my book were within comfortable range of my eye in the chair-car. Before the train started, I was

Confessions of a Best-Seller

given every opportunity to add my own book to my impedimenta.

The sensation awakened by the sight of utter strangers taking up your story, tasting it warily, clinging to it if it be to their liking, or dropping it wearily or contemptuously if it fail to please, is one of the most interesting of the experiences of authorship. On the journey mentioned, one man slept sweetly through what I judged to be the most intense passage in the book; others paid me the tribute of absorbed attention. On the ferry-boat at Jersey City, several copies of the book were interposed between seemingly enchanted readers and the towers and spires of the metropolis. No one, I am sure,will deny to such a poor worm as I the petty joys of popular recognition. To see one's tale on many counters, to hear one's name and titles recited on boats and trains, to find in mid-ocean that your works go with you down to the sea in ships, to see the familiar cover smiling welcome on the table of an obscure foreign inn, — surely the most grudging critic would not deprive a writer of these rewards and delights.

Confessions of a Best-Seller

There is also that considerable army of readers who write to an author in various keys of condemnation or praise. I have found my correspondence considerably augmented by the large sales of a book. There are persons who rejoice to hold before your eyes your inconsistences; or who test you, to your detriment, in the relentless scale of fact. Some one in the Connecticut hills once criticized severely my use of "that" and "which," — a case where an effort at precision was the offense, — and I was involved, before I knew it, in a long correspondence. I have several times been taken severely to task by foes of tobacco for permitting my characters to smoke. Wine, I have found, should be administered to one's characters sparingly, and one's hero must never produce a flask except for restorative uses, — after, let us say, a wild gallop, by night, in the teeth of a storm to relieve a beleaguered citadel, or when the heroine has been rescued at great peril from the clutch of the multitudinous sea. Those strange spirits who pour out their souls in anonymous letters have not ignored me. I salute them with much courtesy, and wish them

233

Confessions of a Best-Seller

well of the gods. Young ladies whose names I
have inadvertently applied to my heroines
have usually dealt with me in agreeable fashion.
The impression that authors have an unlimited
supply of their own wares to give away is responsible for the importunity of managers of
church fairs, philanthropic institutions, and the
like, who assail one cheerfully through the
mails. Before autograph-hunters I have always
been humble; I have felt myself honored by
their attentions; and in spite of their dread
phrase, "Thanking you in advance," — which
might be the shibboleth of their fraternity, from
its prevalence, — I greet them joyfully, and
never filch their stamps.

Now, after all, could anything be less harmful
than my tales? The casual meeting of my hero
and heroine in the first chapter has always been
marked by the gravest circumspection. My
melodrama has never been offensively gory, —
in fact, I have been ridiculed for my bloodless
combats. My villains have been the sort that
anyone with any kind of decent bringing-up
would hiss. A girl in white, walking beside a
lake, with a blue parasol swinging back of her

Confessions of a Best-Seller

head, need offend no one. That the young man emerging from the neighboring wood should not recognize her at once as the young woman ordained in his grandfather's will as the person he must marry to secure the estate, seems utterly banal, I confess; but it is the business of romance to maintain illusions. Realism, with the same agreed state of facts, recognizes the girl immediately — and spoils the story. Or I might put it thus: in realism, much or all is obvious in the first act; in romance, nothing is .quite clear until the third. This is why romance is more popular than realism, for we are all children and want to be surprised. Why villains should always be so stupid, and why heroines should so perversely misunderstand the noble motives of heroes, are questions I cannot answer. Likewise before dear old Mistaken Identity — the most venerable impostor in the novelist's cabinet — I stand dumbly grateful.

On the stage, where a plot is most severely tested, but where the audience must, we are told, always be in the secret, we see constantly how flimsy a mask the true prince need wear. And the reason for this lies in the primal and —

Confessions of a Best-Seller

let us hope — eternal childlikeness of the race. The Zeitgeist will not grind us underfoot so long as we are capable of joy in make-believe, and can renew our youth in the frolics of Peter Pan.

You, sir, who re-read "The Newcomes" every year, and you, madam, reverently dusting your Jane Austen, I am sadder than you can be that my talent is so slender; but is it not a fact that you have watched me at my little tricks on the mimic stage, and been just a little astonished when the sparrow, and not the dove, emerged from the handkerchief? But you prefer the old writers; and so, dear friends, do I!

Having, as I have confessed, deliberately tried my hand at romance merely to see whether I could swim the moat under a cloud of the enemy's arrows, and to gain experience in the mechanism of story-writing, I now declare (though with no illusion as to the importance of the statement) that I have hung my sword over the fireplace; that I shall not again thunder upon the tavern door at midnight; that not much fine gold could tempt me to seek, by means however praiseworthy, to bring that girl

Confessions of a Best-Seller

with the blue parasol to a proper appreciation of the young gentleman with the suit-case, who even now is pursuing her through the wood to restore her lost handkerchief. It has been pleasant to follow the bright guidon of romance; even now, from the window of the tall office-building in which I close these reflections, I can hear the bugles blowing and look upon

"Strangest skies and unbeholden seas."

But I feel reasonably safe from temptation. Little that men do is, I hope, alien to me; and the life that surges round me, and whose sounds rise from the asphalt below, or the hurrying feet on the tiles in my own corridor of this steel-boned tower, — the faint tinkle of telephones, the click of elevator doors, — these things, and the things they stand for, speak with deep and thrilling eloquence; and he who would serve best the literature of his time and country will not ignore them.

THE END